WINNING
FIELD HOCKEY
FOR GIRLS

WINNING
FIELD HOCKEY
FOR GIRLS

BECKY SWISSLER

Foreword by
TRACEY BELBIN

Head Coach
U.S. Women's National Team

A MOUNTAIN LION BOOK

Checkmark Books®

An imprint of Facts On File, Inc.

WINNING FIELD HOCKEY FOR GIRLS

Checkmark Books
An imprint of Facts On File, Inc.
132 West 31st Street
New York NY 10001

Library of Congress Cataloging-in-Publication Data

Swissler, Becky.
　　Winning field hockey for girls / Becky Swissler.
　　　　p. cm.
　　"A Mountain Lion book."
　　Includes bibliographical references.
　　ISBN 0-8160-4724-3 (HC)—ISBN 0-8160-4725-1 (PB)
　　1. Field hockey for girls. I. Title.

　　GV1017.H7 S95 2003
　　796.355'082—dc21　　　　　　　　　　　2002005990

Checkmark Books are available at special discounts when purchased in bulk quantities for businesses, associations, institutions, or sales promotions. Please call our Special Sales Department in New York at (212) 967-8800 or (800) 322-8755.

You can find Facts On File on the World Wide Web at
http://www.factsonfile.com

Text design by Erika K. Arroyo
Cover design by Nora Wertz

Printed in the United States of America

VB FOF 10 9 8 7 6 5 4 3

This book is printed on acid-free paper.

To my sister Amy, who has taught me many valuable lessons in life—one of which was field hockey.

CONTENTS

FOREWORD

Of all the wonderful memories I have of playing world-class field hockey, one magic moment stands out. It occurred when I was playing in the semifinal match for the Australian national team against the Netherlands (Holland) in the 1988 Olympics in Seoul, Korea. Our team went into that game needing a victory over Holland to land us in the gold-medal game.

It was a hard-fought match throughout. I made a run down the right side of the field and executed a perfect dodge that cleared a lane to pass the ball to my teammate. I placed the ball perfectly on her stick, and she slammed the ball past the diving goalie into the net.

Playing for my country was what I'd always dreamed about as a young player, and making the game-winning pass, run, or dodge is the ultimate. When the go-ahead goal came to rest in the netting I was so excited that I could hardly breathe. I hugged my teammates and jumped for joy. It was awesome.

I had practiced the run, dodge, and pass thousands and thousands of times—by myself, in team drills, and over and over in my mind. Those long hours of practice had paid off. In front of thousands in the Olympic stadium and millions on television we went on to win the semifinal game 3-1 and got to play for the gold medal (which we won).

My journey to Olympic gold started many years before in my native Australia when I began playing the game at age four. I followed two older sisters through Australia's women's field hockey development program, playing the game at the club, city, region, state, and national or Olympic level. Field hockey wasn't the only sport that I played—I also played softball, basketball, and tennis through the age of 12—but I knew that field hockey was my favorite, my first love. By age 14 I had reached the national squad and was its youngest member.

Even though I'd made the national squad, my game needed work, and playing with older, more experienced players soon exposed my shortcomings. For one, I found that I could not pass the ball as crisply and accurately as my teammates. It was a weakness that I needed to correct, a skill I needed to improve if I wanted to crack the starting lineup. I set aside two hours a day to practice my passing on my own. I found a wall and hit hundreds of balls against it, concentrating on each stroke until I could hit my target every time.

My hands blistered and bled, but after two weeks of extra practice I showed improvement. It wasn't long before I was consistently passing as forcefully and accurately as my teammates. This taught me a valuable lesson, which I have shared with every team that I coached: To improve you must set a goal and work hard. There are no shortcuts.

From the time I began playing field hockey until I made the Olympic team I had the best coaching that was available. Not everyone is so fortunate, but anyone can study and apply the instruction in this book, *Winning Field Hockey for Girls*. It will not only help you learn what you need to be a step ahead of your opponents, it will also open the way for you to master the skills that will allow you to be the best you can be.

Winning Field Hockey for Girls can help players and coaches at every level establish good fundamentals and improve the overall quality of their play. The importance of learning the fundamentals cannot be understated.

However, field hockey is more than X's and O's, dodges and cuts. This great game is also about learning about how to compete, how to work together, and how to achieve a common goal—valuable skills on and off the field—and *Winning Field Hockey for Girls* will help you tap into these important skills.

Anyone who wants to learn how to play field hockey can study this book, read it closely, and return to its pages whenever you need to refresh your memory. *Winning Field Hockey for Girls* answers questions that aspiring players and coaches have about how to play the game and how to get better. It also helps you to attain your personal goals, realize your greatest dreams, have a lot of fun, and build a lifetime of memories just like I have.

—Tracey Belbin, Head Coach
U.S. Women's National Team

ACKNOWLEDGMENTS

Special thanks to field hockey head coach Charlene Morett and goalie coach Jon O'Haire of Penn State; to UNC head coach Karen Shelton; and to James Madison University's Sally Northcroft for taking the time to share their advice for aspiring players. I also want to thank my family, friends, and boyfriend for being so encouraging and supportive during this project; and a gigantic "Thank you" to Mark Gola, from whom I have learned so much!

INTRODUCTION

In seventh grade I tried out for the soccer team. It didn't take long for me to realize that I was not a soccer player. My older sister, a sophomore in high school and a field hockey player, was offended that I hadn't chosen her sport. I tried to explain to her that I was afraid of the field hockey ball, but she wouldn't hear it.

Every day for one year she took me into the backyard and taught me the fundamentals of the game. We drove the ball back and forth across the yard, moving farther apart from each other each day until we reached the limits of our yard. She explained to me what the positions were and how they all worked together to form a team. She set up cones for me to dribble through. She made me flick and scoop the ball over garbage cans in the yard. She outlined a goal on our woodpile so I would have a target to shoot at when I played by myself. The following year I tried out for the field hockey team and never looked back.

Just Like the Backyard

In this book you will find exactly what I found in my sister. Although this book is slightly more formal and (sorry, Amy) much more knowledgeable, the idea is basically the same. Both players and coaches will find something worthwhile here—be it the drills at the end of each chapter or the advice from successful Division I field hockey coaches who had plenty of tips to share. Along with a short history of the sport and a breakdown of the rules of the game, the early chapters of the book begin with the more fundamental skills: proper grip, proper stance, dribbling, passing, and receiving. As the book progresses, so do the topics—concluding with offensive and defensive team strategies. A separate chapter is devoted to goalie play and equipment.

As with any sport, the most important thing to do before playing is to get your body in shape. An entire chapter is dedicated to conditioning your body so you won't be sore or injure yourself when you start playing.

Taking It to the Field

It is important that you have a physical understanding of each topic discussed in this book, as well as a mental one. Go out onto the hockey field, or into the backyard, and apply the knowledge you gain as you read so that you have a full mental and physical understanding of the game. Practice, practice, practice!

The most important thing is that you have fun with the sport. Read, learn, apply, and relax. This is a sport to enjoy!

HISTORY, RULES, AND EQUIPMENT

1

HISTORY

While field hockey is merely a century old in the United States, it dates back nearly 4,000 years. Drawings of men holding curved sticks with a ball on the ground were found in the Egyptian tomb of Beni-Hasan in the Nile Valley. Many believe that these drawings offer evidence that some form of field hockey was played by the Egyptians, Greeks, and Romans.

Field hockey was developed and popularized in Europe. The first field hockey club was established in the British Isles in 1849. By 1876, a collection of clubs in England formed the Hockey Union. The Hockey Union created a set of rules to regulate the sport and organize fair competition. Those rules and regulations provided the foundation by which the game is played today.

During the late 19th century in Europe, women actively sought greater opportunities to develop mentally and physically as individuals. The late-Victorian physical fitness movement associated health and good looks with exercise. Women began viewing exercise as a desirable undertaking. In addition, at this time women started attending college in large numbers.

The increase in physical activity among women combined with their gathering in numbers at college created an environment in need of a women's sport. Although field hockey was then a sport played exclusively by men, the game was introduced to women and they took to it quickly. It was the first team sport considered proper for women and finally allowed them an opportunity to exercise in a competitive atmosphere. Between 1887 and 1900, women's field hockey associations were established in Ireland, England, Scotland, and Wales.

Women's field hockey spread to Australia, New Zealand, South Africa, Canada, and the United States in the early 20th century. In 1901, a British physical education instructor named Constance Applebee staged a field hockey exhibition at Harvard University. Applebee would later become known as "Miss Hockey" in the United States. She spent two years teaching and promoting the game to northeastern colleges and by 1922, helped create the U.S. Field Hockey Association (USFHA). The popularity of field hockey continued to spread with Applebee's efforts, and she helped establish the International Federation of Women's Hockey Associations (IFWHA) in 1927.

A Field Hockey Star Is Born

As is often the case with athletics in the United States, a new sport sometimes does not catch on with youth until an individual player is established as a star. Beth Anders, born in 1953 in Norristown, Pennsylvania, was the key member of the U.S. national team from 1969 through 1984. She played in 13 World Cup tournaments and was the U.S. leader on and off the field. Anders was an exceptional scorer and has been a successful collegiate coach at Old Dominion University in

More than 100,000 girls play competitive field hockey in the United States today.

Norfolk, Virginia. She is the most prominent field hockey figure the United States has ever known.

Men's field hockey became an Olympic sport in 1908, but it was not until 1980 that field hockey became an official Olympic sport for women. Unfortunately for Anders and her U.S. teammates, the United States boycotted the 1980 Moscow Olympics. Their Olympic debut would have to wait four more years.

At the 1984 Summer Olympics in Los Angeles, the U.S. team stunned the field hockey world by earning a bronze medal in their first Olympic appearance. Women's field hockey was now firmly ensconced as an American sport and now had an Olympic medal to prove it.

The early 1980s also marked a time of growth for women's field hockey in collegiate athletics. For the first time in 1981, the National Collegiate Athletic Association (NCAA) sanctioned a field hockey tournament to crown a national champion. The University of Connecticut won the first-ever Division I field hockey national championship in 1981. Northeastern schools have dominated the national titles since, with Old Dominion University (coached by Beth Anders) leading the way with nine national crowns. There are signs, however, of elite field hockey programs developing across the country. In 2001, the University of Michigan won its first NCAA Division I national championship by defeating the University of Maryland 2-0.

Today, more than 100,000 girls play field hockey as a competitive sport. More than 98 percent of those players are under the age of 21. In 2001, 5,203 student-athletes played field hockey at colleges and universities across the country.

EQUIPMENT

The Field

The playing field measures 100 yards long by 60 yards wide. Standing in the middle of each end line is a goal cage. Each goal cage is seven feet high by 12 feet wide. Most goals use a mesh netting to enclose the cage.

There is a 25-yard line from each end of the field and a 50-yard line at midfield. This divides the field into four sections. A semicircle, called the striking circle, arcs out in front of the goal. The apex of the semicircle is 16 yards from the center point of the goal line, and its diameter runs 32 yards in length along the goal line. Corner hit lines intersect with the goal line within five yards of each corner flag.

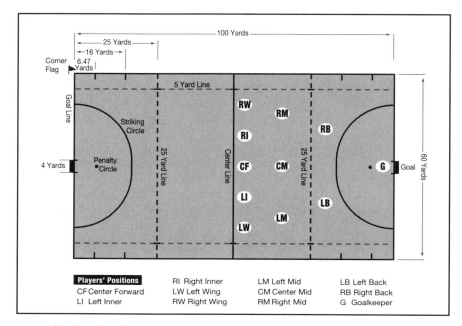

A standard hockey field. This is one of many formations implemented by field hockey coaches.

Uniforms

Today's field hockey uniform may not be to your liking, but years ago American women players were forced to dress in long-sleeved flannel shirts and corduroy skirts that hung six inches from the ground. The uniforms today, which consist of a short-sleeved shirt and a short skirt called a kilt, are much more comfortable for competition.

Wear a shirt with a uniform number on the front and back. The number allows the referee to distinguish between one player and the next. Most girls wear sliding pants beneath their kilt to protect them from

In order to get on the field and display your skills, you've got to wear the proper uniform and equipment.

cuts and scrapes when sliding or diving for balls. For footwear, wear a pair of lightweight leather shoes with cleats. Cleats are essential for attaining good traction when running, cutting, stopping, and starting. Sweaters, gloves, headbands, high socks, and tights are useful when dressing for cold weather.

Protective Gear

Flying balls and sticks can result in a lot of bumps and bruises. It's best to protect yourself with gear to minimize potential injuries. Shin guards must be worn at all times in practice and games. Besides protecting yourself, you'll feel more secure wearing shin guards, enabling you to play more aggressively. Mouthpieces are also required to protect your mouth and teeth from aerial balls and high-flying sticks and elbows.

Goalies must wear full mask helmets, and they must include a throat guard. Gloves, chest protectors, and leg pads protect the body from fast-traveling shots. Goalies also wear padded, squared-off overshoes so they can kick the ball without risk of injury.

Stick and Ball

Most sticks are between 34 and 36 inches long and weigh 17 to 19 ounces. They must not exceed 28 ounces nor be less than 12 ounces. Choose a stick that suits your individual height and strength. The sticks are made of wood and have rounded backs and handles. The stick's curved end, called the blade, has a flat left side. This is the only part of the stick with which you're allowed to hit the ball. The head of the stick cannot have any metal fittings, sharp edges, or splinters.

The ball has a hard outer shell of white leather. This protects the ball's interior of cork and twine. Balls weigh $5^1/2$ to $5^3/4$ ounces and have a circumference of $8^{13}/16$ to $9^1/4$ inches.

Balls must be played with the flat side of the stick.

THE GAME

Field hockey is a game in which two teams of 11 players use a stick with a hook at the end to hit a ball along the ground. The object of the game is to hit the ball into the opponent's goal. The team that scores the most goals wins the game.

To score, the ball must be hit or deflected by an offensive player who is standing inside the striking circle. High school games consist of two 30-minute periods. Collegiate and international games have two 35-minute periods.

THE RULES

Starting Play

The game is started by a pass back. It is made at the center of the field to start the game, at the beginning of the second half, and also after each goal is scored. All players must stand in their positions on their half of the field and must be at least five yards from the ball. The ball is pushed or hit backward and must not cross over the center line.

Scoring

A goal is scored when the entire ball crosses over the goal line between the posts and under the crossbar. The ball must be played by an attacker standing inside the striking circle. However, the goal is valid if the ball deflects off a defender inside the circle.

Bully

If an incident or injury occurs during regulation play, a bully is played on the spot of the incident's origin. A player from each team stands squarely facing the sidelines. Their own goal line is on their right side. The ball is placed on the ground between the players. Both players tap the ground (on their side of the ball) and then touch sticks (above the ball) three times. After they touch three times—ground, sticks, ground, sticks, ground, sticks—they attempt to hit the ball toward the opposition's goal.

Free Hits

Free hits are awarded when an infringement by the opposing team has occurred. The ball is placed at the spot of the infringement and is hit or pushed by a striker. No player on the opposing team is permitted to be within five yards of the striker. The striker may not touch the ball a second time until another player contacts the ball. (In other words, you're not allowed to dribble the ball off a free hit.)

Long Hits

Corner hits are taken by the offense on the end line within five yards of the corner flag. They are awarded to the offensive team when the defensive team unintentionally hits the ball over its defensive end line from within the 25-yard line. The player taking the corner hit may push or hit the ball but may not touch or be within reach of the ball until another player contacts the ball.

Penalty Corners

When a defensive player deliberately hits a ball over the end line or fouls a player without preventing a goal from being scored, a penalty corner is awarded to the offense. The ball is placed on the end line 10 yards from the goalpost. A maximum of five defensive players are allowed to stand behind the end line (including goalie). The rest of the defensive team must stand behind the 50-yard line. No defensive player is permitted to cross the end line or center line until the ball is struck.

The offensive players must stand outside the striking circle. The receiver must receive the ball and stop it completely outside the circle. Once the ball is struck, they may charge toward the goal cage.

Penalty Stroke

A penalty stroke is awarded to the attacking team if a defensive player inside the circle commits an intentional foul or an unintentional foul that prevents a goal. The stroke is taken by an attacker from a spot seven yards in front of the center of the goal. The attacker may push, scoop, or flick the ball toward the goal. The goaltender must stand on the end goal line and may not move her feet or position until the ball has been played.

16-Yard Hits

Should the attacking team send the ball over the end line, the game shall be restarted by a 16-yard hit. It shall be taken opposite the place where the ball crossed the end line and up to 16 yards from the inner edge of the end line. Legal strokes are a drive or push, and the opponent must be at least five yards away from the striker.

Side In

When a team hits the ball out of bounds along the sideline, a side in is given to the other team. For a side in, opponents must be at least five

There are all types of drills and games that help improve your stick handling skills. Here, two girls are stick juggling.

yards from the player taking the hit. She must either push or drive the ball back into play.

Fouls

Free hits are awarded for various rule violations (fouls). Below is a list of offenses that will force the referee to blow her whistle and grant a free hit for the opposing team. Fouls that occur outside the striking circle result in free hits taken at the point of the foul. If the attacking team commits a foul inside the striking circle, the defense may take its free hit from anywhere opposite the violation up to 16 yards from the inner edge of the end line.

- Hitting the ball with the round side of the stick
- Tripping, pushing, or striking a player
- Playing the ball while you are on the ground
- Shielding the ball from an opponent with your body or stick
- Interfering with an opponent's stick
- Undercutting or raising the ball dangerously
- Deliberately/blindly hitting into an opponent

- Using your foot or leg to support your stick when tackling an opponent
- Using anything other than the stick to move the ball downfield
- Lifting the stick over your head or striking a ball that travels above shoulder height
- Intentionally stopping or slowing a ball with any body part
- Deliberately removing required equipment or wearing/using illegal equipment
- Placing the ball after a hand stop of an aerial ball by the goaltender

Goaltender

The goalie has the job of preventing the ball from going into her team's cage. She is the only player who can use any part of her body to stop the ball. She cannot catch the ball but can use her hands to stop the ball and drop it to her feet. Goalies are permitted to kick the ball within the striking circle and use this privilege frequently to clear the ball away from the goal cage. Once they leave the circle, the same rules apply to them as to the field players.

2
UNDERSTANDING THE BASICS: BODY POSITIONING AND GRIP

"In this sport when we see games break down, it's because the fundamentals have failed."

—Charlene Morett, head coach at Penn State University

The fundamental skills of field hockey—dribbling, passing, receiving, shooting, and tackling—are extremely important to every player at every position. In order to execute those skills correctly and consistently, your body must assume the proper position. Several of the following chapters will discuss these skills in detail, but this chapter will focus on the way your body must prepare itself to perform those skills. The newspaper might clamor about the game-winning goal you scored in overtime, but in order to make that heroic shot, you've got to be set in the right position.

Not much comes naturally when learning to play field hockey. It takes time to become comfortable with the positioning of your body and the fact that you're manipulating a foreign object (the ball) with a stick. By training your body to perform properly from day one, you'll avoid developing poor habits that would eventually need to be corrected. Concentrate on perfecting your field hockey skills first, and in time your comfort level in performing those skills will rise. There are no shortcuts to developing proper technique. It takes practice, patience, and perseverance.

Every skill in field hockey—dribbling, passing, shooting, and tackling—begins with balance and proper positioning.

Consider each lesson outlined in this chapter to be a letter in the alphabet. No single lesson is more important than another, but each is essential to understanding the big picture. In the end, it's these basic principles that will allow you to evolve into the best player you're capable of becoming.

Just as we learn the alphabet letter by letter before we can read or write, there are certain fundamentals in field hockey that must be learned before you can adequately play the game. In its most basic form, the foundation of field hockey rests on the relationship between the stick, your body, and the ball. Footwork and balance are the groundwork for those basics.

"I think in high school coaches move away from the fundamentals too soon," says Sally Northcroft, assistant coach at James Madison University in Harrisonburg, Virginia. "It may seem kind of boring and mundane, but it's so important for beginners to really understand and learn the basics of the game."

Learn all the basics and recognize how they'll influence the rest of your game. Once you accept the age-old adage that you must learn to walk before you can run, you'll build a solid foundation from which your abilities to pass, receive, dribble, dodge, shoot, and tackle will evolve.

PICKING UP THE STICK

The most common mistake a beginner makes when picking up a field hockey stick is to grip it like a bat. This is a habit you've got to break immediately. "I've had kids holding their sticks like baseball and softball bats and they're convinced it's the only way to hold it," Coach Northcroft complains.

The home grip for holding the field hockey stick is the "shake hands grip." From this grip, you can execute any skill or technique in

Reach out with your left hand as if you're about to shake someone's hand. Grab the top handle of the stick so your hand is aligned with the inside edge of the stick.

Notice the V shape formed by the thumb and index finger of each hand on the stick.

hockey. If you grip the stick incorrectly it will prove detrimental to all of your basic skills.

To set up your grip, position the stick on the ground so the toe is pointing straight up to the sky and the stick is on its outside edge where the rounded side meets the flat side. Reach out your left hand as if you're about to shake hands. (Ignore the fact that we use our right hands to shake hands for just one moment.) Now instead of grabbing onto someone's hand, shake the top handle of the stick. The V formed by your thumb and pointer finger of your left hand is in line with the inside edge of the stick. The inside of the stick is the side that the hook, or toe, curves toward. Now reach out to shake the stick with your right hand (keeping your left hand on the stick). Place the right hand $5^1/2$ to seven inches below the left. The V formed by your right hand is also directly in line with the inside edge of the stick. The head of the stick is pointing forward and slightly to your right, with the toe pointing up. The flat side is facing to the left.

Hold the stick comfortably with both hands in front of you and away from your body. Stand with your feet shoulder width apart and bend your knees until the toe of the stick is on the ground. Your left hand controls the stick and all of its movements, while your right hand acts as a guide for the stick.

Reverse Grip

Use the reverse grip when the ball is on your left side. From the shake hands position, loosen your right hand so it can guide the stick as it moves. Turn your left hand to the left as if you were opening a book. Your left elbow is now tucked inside next to your rib cage, and the

When the ball moves to the left side of your body, use the reverse grip to play the ball.

inside of your left wrist is facing up. Your right arm crosses in front of your body. The stick is now positioned to the left of your body with the flat side facing to the right and the toe pointing toward you.

Once the stick reaches the reverse position, retighten your right-hand grip. The V formed by your right thumb and index finger points directly down the outside edge of the stick.

Always keep your fingers together when holding the stick in a firm shake hands grip. A common mistake is to extend the index or pointer finger down the stick. This exposes that finger to being hit by another stick or by the ball. Keep your fingers together to avoid risking an injury.

USFHA

U.S. Field Hockey Association (USFHA) is the national governing body for the sport in the United States. The USFHA is a member of the U.S. Olympic Committee (USOC), the Fédération Internationale de Hockey (FIH), and the Pan American Hockey Federation.

The mission of the USFHA is to create a learning and supportive environment for amateur players; to provide players, coaches, officials, and administrators with various opportunities in the sport; to prepare teams for competition in the Olympic Games, the Pan American Games, and other USOC- and FIH-sponsored events; and to serve as ambassadors of goodwill while representing the United States domestically and internationally.

The USFHA provides programs to players of all ages to continue developing their skills in the sport. The most recognized youth programs include Futures, Super Camp, and the Junior Olympics. For more information about these and other USFHA programs, visit www.usfieldhockey.com.

If you notice that you often lose possession of the ball, move your hands farther apart for greater control. Conversely, if your stick handling is too slow, move your hands closer together to speed up your movements. Establish control with the ball first, before working on speed. The latter will come with time.

BALANCE IN YOUR STANCE

A proper field hockey stance is similar to an athletic stance in basketball, tennis, and soccer. Stand with your feet slightly wider than shoulder width apart. Keep your weight on the balls of your feet. Bend at your knees, but not so far that when you look down you can't see your toes. Stick your rear end out as if you're about to sit down and bend at your hips. Bending your body in this way lowers your center of gravity, which increases your balance. Balance is incredibly important to the game of field hockey because every movement is quick and precise. Keep your head up and your arms out, holding the stick in the shake hands grip.

Practice shifting your weight from one foot to the other. Change the pace of your shifts to get comfortable holding your body weight on the balls of your feet, all the while staying low to the ground and balanced.

Offensive Stance

Hold the stick in the shake hands grip. Position your body in the balanced stance described above, bending your knees and waist until the toe of your stick touches the ground. Keep your head up and your arms and stick out in front of you. This is an attack stance. Familiarize yourself with this position and body posture—it is the cornerstone for every dribbling, dodging, passing, and shooting technique you will use in field hockey.

As an offensive player, you have the advantage of knowing

Holding your stick out in front of you, position your feet slightly farther than shoulder width apart, flex the knees, and bend at the waist. Always keep your weight on the balls of your feet to maintain balance.

where and what you're going to do with the ball. Glance down at the ball to maintain its whereabouts but keep your head up so you can see the field and your teammates. If there is open space, an open teammate, or a defensive player approaching, you won't know it unless you pick your head up to see it.

Defensive Stance

With the stick in the shake hands grip, stand in the balanced stance described above. Bend deeper at your knees to lower your center of gravity. When playing defense, it is important for you to stay low to the ground and keep your stick on the ground to stop the ball.

Hold the stick in the shake hands grip with the toe of your stick off to your right side and the flat side of the stick facing forward. Drop your right hand lower on the stick for greater control. Your left foot is slightly ahead of your right. The left foot is the natural lead foot in field hockey, so the stick is positioned to play the ball on your right side. Keep your weight on the balls of your feet.

The defensive player (left) drops her right hand lower on the stick and bends deeper at the knees to lower her center of gravity.

MOVING THE BALL

The ball belongs on the toe of your stick, cradled between the ground and the stick. Imagine there's a magnetic force connecting your body, the stick, and the ball that allows everything to move as one when dribbling down the field.

Control Box

The first step in dribbling is to determine the appropriate distance your body should be from the ball. To get a feel for this, hold the ball in your left hand. Stand with your feet slightly wider than shoulder width apart and squat down, extending your left arm in front of you.

When you can reach no farther without losing balance, place the ball on the ground. Without moving your feet, stand up and hold the stick in the shake hands grip. Stand in an offensive position with your head up and your upper body square to the ball. "Square" means that you are facing an object straight on, and that object is centered in the middle of your chest so both shoulders are facing it.

Using the shake hands grip, extend the stick out so its flat

To determine how far to play the ball from your body, hold the ball in your left hand (above). Flex at the knees, bend at the waist, and extend your arm out in front of you. Drop the ball straight to the ground (bottom left).

The control box is the area in which you have the greatest control as a dribbler.

side touches the right side of the ball. This is your natural dribbling distance from the ball. Create an imaginary line that runs through the ball, parallel to your feet. With your stick, push the ball along that imaginary line to the left until the ball is in front of your left foot. Now switch to the reverse grip and pull the ball with the reverse stick back along the imaginary line until the ball is in front of your right foot. This area is called the control box because it is the area in which you, as a dribbler, have the greatest control of the ball.

FOOTWORK

Footwork is equally important to proper positioning in field hockey. Balance and footwork go hand in hand—or foot in foot. Staying low and on your toes improves your balance. Karen Shelton, head coach at the University of North Carolina, says, "It is imperative that you move your feet at all times. It allows you to be quick and agile under any circumstances."

If the ball is moving, even if the action is on the other side of the field, you should be moving too. Making runs without the ball on offense creates space for your teammates. Constantly reposition yourself so you're ready to play when the ball comes your way. Field hockey is a fast game, and if you don't keep moving, it will pass you by.

At times, play can get congested. When you pull up to some traffic, take short, quick steps. Anticipate where the ball is going and move in that direction, but be ready to change your direction at any time if the ball is intercepted or redirected. There are several footwork techniques to learn, but most are based on common sense, so just use your head— or your feet.

OFFENSIVE FOOTWORK

Footwork is the most important aspect of executing offensive moves. Use your feet to fake out defenders, stop and start, accelerate, and slow down. Developing quick and nimble feet will improve your play.

Breaking Down Your Steps

The law of inertia (a body in motion stays in motion) states that it is impossible to stop on a dime once you are in motion. Breaking down your steps allows you to slow down and gain control of your movements. If you are breaking down your steps because you are chasing a free ball, shorten your strides when you come within five yards of the ball. Move into an offensive position with two hands on the stick in a shake hands grip. Get your body under control so you can take possession of the ball.

If you are speed dribbling with the ball and you see a defender ahead, break down your steps as you approach her. To fake out or dribble past a defender, you must be able to accelerate. You can't accelerate if you're running at full speed. Begin breaking down your steps when you are about 10 yards from your opponent.

Slow down the speed of the ball so it matches the speed at which you are traveling. On a natural grass field, this is not so difficult. On artificial surfaces, however, the ball moves very quickly and you will often find yourself sprinting to keep up with it. To slow the ball, position your stick so it is ahead of the ball with the flat side facing the ball. Turn your left hand as if you're executing a reverse grip switch, but keep the stick in front of and to the right of your right foot near the ball. As you break down your steps, cradle the ball, using the stick as a brake.

Changing Speed

When a defender is marking you, mix up the speed of your movements. While running around the field, change your pace from a jog to a sprint to a stride, or any combination thereof. If you are moving at top speed, switch gears to half that pace and then accelerate to 75 percent of your full speed.

Keep your weight on the balls of your feet when you're changing speeds. With only the balls of your feet touching the ground, you can break down steps, cut your stride in half, and pick up speed smoothly. To accelerate, dig into the ground with the balls of your feet as you take off. To slow down, elevate your posture, pump your knees, and land with your weight on the balls of your feet. If you always pump your knees hard—whether sprinting, jogging, or slowing down—it will be difficult for the defender to determine your speed by observation.

Constantly altering your speed tires out your defender and makes it difficult for her to judge an appropriate distance to play from you. As a general rule, if you're a faster player, the defense gives you more room so they have more time to react to you. If you're slower, however, chances are they'll guard you tight. But if your pace is constantly changing, your opponent will be unable to determine how to defend you. Only you know what you're about to do, leaving her unable to anticipate and reduced to simply reacting.

Changing Direction

Another offensive strategy influenced by footwork is changing direction. Much like changing speeds, it's to your advantage that only you know what you're going to do next. All the defensive player can do is react.

Changing direction can be used on its own or with a change in speed. If you are running straight down the field, shorten your strides to get your body under control. When you are ready to change direction, place all your weight on the ball of the foot opposite of the direction you want to go.

If you want to move to the right, push off the outside of your left foot and turn your upper body to the right. Then step to the right with your right foot. Pick up speed as you take off. Continue doing this to zigzag. This tires out and confuses the defense.

Throw a Body Fake

The body fake is basically a combination of a change in speed and direction. This technique is great when you want to lose your defender and cut toward the ball to receive a pass. Use your feet and upper body to fake in one direction and then explode in a different direction. Basketball, football, and soccer players also use this type of move.

Begin the fake by breaking down your strides. Step hard on the ball of the foot that is the direction you are faking. For example, if you are faking left, step to the left with your left foot. Point your toes to the left and indicate with your head and shoulders that your body is going

To fake left, plant your weight on your left leg and lean forward to that side. If the defender shifts her weight to defend that direction, she's susceptible to the opposite side.

to go to the left. Your upper body is integral to selling the fake. Also, focus your eyes on the direction you are faking.

Square your shoulders so they are in line with where your foot is pointing and pump your upper body and head in that direction. Before committing your body entirely to the left, pull back and push off the outside of your left foot to the right. Step with your right foot to the right and dig down with the ball of your foot into the ground to accelerate. If your defender leans even slightly to the fake side, she'll be off-balance and unable to keep up with you when you accelerate to the opposite side.

DEFENSIVE FOOTWORK

As a defender, always keep your opponent in front of you. If you follow this rule religiously, you'll be a great defender. When marking (defending) an offensive player, take quick, short steps to stay with the opponent. Taking shorter strides allows you to be ready to move with your opponent and react to any change in direction she might make. Don't fall back on your heels. It puts you in an unbalanced position, making it easy for your opponent to burst past you. One defensive trick to remember is that you do not want to be watching your opponent's feet or upper body. A good offensive player uses those areas for body fakes. She'll try to make you commit to one direction and then will quickly move past you in the other direction. When defending, keep your eye on the midsection—the belly button—of your opponent. This keeps you with your opponent and prevents you from falling for fakes and overcommitting.

Breaking Down Your Steps

Remember the principle of inertia. In order to pose a defensive threat after sprinting after the ball or an opponent, shorten your stride to control your body and all of your movements. Begin breaking down your steps as you come within five yards of the opponent. Slow yourself down by landing each stride on the balls of your feet instead of on the heel as you do in a normal sprint. Pump your knees high as well. Landing on the balls of your feet and pumping your knees acts as a brake on your body, allowing you to regain control of your movements and get in a position to play the ball. Lower your body so you are closer to the ground with two hands on your stick, resting it on the ground.

Judge your distance from the opponent to determine when to break down your steps. You want to keep her in front of you and maintain a distance of about one stick length away from the ball, $1^1/2$ stick lengths away from the dribbler. This space gives you time to react to her movements. If you're too close, she'll be able to easily slip past you. Stay poised and balanced and keep your opponent in front of you. From this position, you can extend your stick and make contact with the ball when it comes off the dribbler's stick. This is called tackling and will be discussed in greater detail in chapter 6, Tackling.

Lead Foot

As a defender, always establish your lead foot. The lead foot keeps you balanced so you can move forward, backward, or to either side. It also forces the offense to move in the direction of your choice.

Maintain a distance of about one stick length from the ball, about $1^1/2$ stick lengths from your opponent. Face the dribbler with your back to the goal cage you are defending, keeping her closer to the outside of the field. Your lead foot is the opposite foot of the direction you want to force your opponent. You always want to force her away from the goal you are defending and toward the nearest sideline. If you are defending on the right side of the field, for example, establishing a left lead foot will force your opponent to stay toward the right (her left), the outside of the field. Never let the ball move past your lead foot.

When your opponent is dribbling down the left side of the field, lead with your right foot. If she's dribbling down the right side, lead with your left foot. This contains her to the sideline and keeps her out of the middle of the field.

Move your feet constantly, repositioning them to keep your opponent in front of you as she dribbles.

If you are defending on the right side of the field, square your shoulders to the dribbler's right shoulder. Keep your stick on the ground at all times and protect your lead foot with your stick so that the dribbler cannot hit the ball into your feet and draw a penalty.

On the left side of the field, your right foot is your lead foot. Square your shoulders to the dribbler's left shoulder. The dribbler will have the ball on her right side. Defensive positioning along the left side of the field is difficult because it is your nonstick side. Give the attacking player a little more space when defending the left side.

Drop Step

When you successfully establish the lead foot, your opponent is forced to move in the direction you want her to go. However, if the dribbler successfully switches directions and moves past your lead foot, use a drop step to recover.

Imagine your left foot is your lead foot and your opponent is to the right of you. She quickly pulls the ball to her right, passing your lead foot and moving to the left of you. You react by taking a drop step. Keep your knees bent and stay low in a defensive position. Swing your left foot back to open your body so it faces your opponent and your right foot is leading. Your shoulders are now square to her left shoulder instead of her right. Keep your stick on the ground and move with her.

If your opponent attempts to dribble past you toward the middle of the field, use a drop step to keep her in front of you.

Sliding and Shuffling

In the above example, when you shift your lead foot and change directions, use a slide, or side-to-side, movement (sometimes called a basketball slide) to stay with the dribbler as she dribbles across the field. Running takes you out of your defensive positioning and presents the dribbler with an opportunity to move around you, but the slide or shuffle keeps you in position.

To stay with speedy attackers, shuffle your feet along with them. Avoid using crossover steps to eliminate the chance of entangling your legs.

Shuffle to the left by pushing off the ball of your right foot and stepping to the left with your left foot. Keep your knees bent and stay low to the ground. Land on the ball of your left foot and pull your right foot in so it is closer to your left. Shift your weight to the ball of your right foot and step out with the left again. Repeat this motion to stay with your opponent as she moves across the field. Use the shuffle to travel from one side to the other without rising out of the defensive position. Keep your stick on the ground and your eyes on the ball.

If you have difficulty keeping up with your opponent when shuffling, leave the defensive position and run. Remember that the golden rule of playing defense is keeping yourself between the goal and your opponent.

Running Backward

There are also times you will have to run backward down the field to keep your opponent in front of you. The only way to gain comfort running backward is to practice. Lift your feet up high so you don't trip. Land on and push off from the balls of your feet.

This is not a speed movement. If you need to catch a sprinting dribbler, turn around and sprint. But if you are repositioning to keep your opponent in front of you, running backward is a sufficient method of getting yourself into position.

ALWAYS REMEMBER THE BASICS

The topics discussed in this chapter are the basic fundamentals of field hockey. That doesn't mean, however, that they are reserved for beginners. It is always a good idea to review the basics so that your overall understanding of the game stays sharp and continues to improve. As mentioned in the beginning, these are the building blocks—the foundation—of the game.

Coach Morett's advice: "Spend time on individual skills and do that repeatedly four or five times a week, 20 or 30 minutes a day, so you develop an idea of how to work the stick and are comfortable with the stick in your hand. Unfortunately, field hockey people think you need a whole team to play, but if you can practice one-on-one skills with a friend, just like one-on-one in basketball, then you can improve your stick skills and confidence with the ball. You'll have fun working the ball and that fun will translate into enhanced skills."

Focus on these basics, and you will improve your passing, receiving, intercepting, shooting, dodging, tackling, and dribbling. If at any time you feel yourself starting to lose your touch or are slumping on the field, go back to the basics. Practice dribbling, quick movements, and balance. Train your mind to visualize body positioning such as the lead foot and forcing your opponent out on the defensive end, and changing direction and body fakes on the offensive end. Review the key components to all the basic skills and you'll soon find yourself back on the path to recovery.

FINAL THOUGHTS:

"Field hockey is such a challenging game, I think the key is to just have a passion for the sport. I've been playing for 30 years and I still enjoy the challenge the stick and ball present to me—and having fun with that challenge. That's how you come to embrace the game. It can be a very frustrating game and the challenge is overcoming that frustration, which enables you to play with skill."

—Charlene Morett, head coach, Penn State University

DRILLS AND GAMES

Indian Dribbling

Players: One
Equipment: Two sticks and one ball
Distance: One stick length

Lay one stick on the ground in front of you and position your body in an offensive dribbling stance with your feet parallel to the stick. Hold the second stick in the offensive shake hands grip. The stick on the ground represents your control box. Now place a ball on the ground next to the end of the stick in front of your right foot on the side of the stick closer to you. Push the ball down the length of the stick until it is at the other end and therefore in front of your left foot. Change to the reverse grip and pull the ball with the reverse stick the length of the stick back to the spot where you started. This is Indian dribbling—one complete dribble is a forehand push and reverse pull up and back the length of the stick. Time yourself for 60 seconds and see how many dribbles you complete. Aim to increase the amount of dribbling every time, but maintain control of the ball.

Red Rover

Players: More than four
Distance: 50 yards

That's right, it's Red Rover—just like you played in elementary school. One person is Red Rover, or "it." The rest of the players (this is a great game with an entire team) line up on the end line. The Red Rover stands on the 25-yard line and shouts, "Red Rover, Red Rover, anyone wearing blue come over." Everyone on the end line who is wearing something blue sprints to the 50-yard line. Note that blue can be substituted with any other physical description—anyone wearing shin guards, a ribbon in their hair, red, and so on.

As the players who are wearing blue sprint across the field, Red Rover runs after them, tagging as many as she can. Whoever she tags joins her in the middle of the field and together they are all "it." Once the group of players wearing blue has made it to the 50 or have been tagged and are "it" on the 25-yard line, Red Rover shouts for any players remaining on the end line wearing some other particular color or style to cross to the 50. The group of players who are "it" all run after the remaining players sprinting across to the 50.

When all players have left the end line, there should be a significant number of "its," as well as a number of players who have successfully crossed to the 50 untagged. Red Rover then calls out another description, forcing the people on the 50-yard line who match that description to sprint back to the end line. The more Red Rovers that get tagged, the more difficult it becomes for the players to sprint across the field safely.

The sprinters must use offensive footwork and body fakes to get away from Red Rover, and the Red Rovers must use defensive tactics and speed to tag the running players. It is balance and footwork broken down, and it's a lot of fun.

Steal the Bacon

Players: At least six
Equipment: Everyone has a stick, one ball, and four cones
Distance: Use the area on the field between the 50- and 25-yard line

Gather a group of at least six together to play this game. An outside source, ideally the coach, splits the group in half. He or she then secretly gives each player a number. The numbers used are equal to the amount of players per side—if there are three girls per team, the numbers one, two, and three are used. The same set of numbers are given to each team, so there are two ones, two twos, and two threes in the entire group.

One team spreads out across the 25-yard line, the other team is on the 50-yard line. The two teams face each other. Place a ball in the middle of the field between the two lines. At each sideline between the 25 and 50, set up two cones about six feet apart as a goal.

The coach calls out an assigned number, and the two people from opposite teams who have that number race to the ball. The players racing to the ball must break down their steps from their sprint to control their bodies as they approach the ball. Whoever gets there first is offense, the second to arrive is defense. Work on positioning and moving with the ball.

To score a point for your team, dribble the ball on your stick through the two cones you are facing. There is no set direction for each side to aim for, whoever gets the ball first decides that by the direction they first dribble in. The team scoring the most goals by drilling through the cones is the winner.

Defending without a Stick

Players: Two
Equipment: Four cones
Distance: A 10-yard square grid

Mark off a 10-yard square grid on the field. One player, the defense, stands in the middle of the grid. The other player, the offense, starts on one of the lines of the square grid. Neither player has a stick. The offense runs into the grid, moving from side to side, forward and backward, trying to fake the defense. Her goal is to pass the defense and come out on the other side of the grid opposite where she started. The defense's job is to keep the offense in front of her, preventing her from getting to the other side.

In this game, the offense must use quick footwork, body fakes, and changes of speed and direction to fool the defense. The defense stands in a defensive position, weight on the balls of your feet, knees bent, hips bent, and hands reaching out in front of you as if you are holding a stick. Move with the offense. The defense will execute drop steps, backpedaling (running backwards), and shuffling to keep the offense in front of her. The key here, the defense will learn, is that watching the offense's feet or upper body will lead you astray. Concentrate on the belly button or midsection of the offense, and you won't fall for any of her fakes.

Defensive Circuit Workout

Players: One to 25
Equipment: Four cones, stick
Distance: 50 yards (half a field)

Place one cone on the corner of the field where the sideline meets the 25-yard line. Another cone is straight up that sideline on the 50-yard line. A third cone is in the middle of the field on the 50-yard line. The fourth cone is in the middle of the field on the 25-yard line. These four cones form one giant square.

Holding your stick in two hands, start at the first cone and sprint to the second cone. When you come within five yards of the second one, break down your steps. Hold the breakdown position in front of the second cone for 10 seconds. This means you are low, your knees are bent, your rear end is sticking out, and your weight is on the balls of your feet. In this position continue running in place on the balls of your feet, staying low and broken down. After 10 seconds, slide down the 50 to the third cone, leading with your right foot. When you reach this cone, drop step back down the middle of the field to the fourth cone. When you drop step, alternate sides with each step and really swing your hips open and step back and out to the side with each step, pivoting off your lead foot. When you reach the fourth cone, backpedal to the end line. After crossing the end line, jog to the first cone and continue the circuit.

This is a good drill for teams. When the first player finishes breaking down her steps at the second cone and begins shuffling, the second player can take off so everyone is always moving.

Offensive Circuit Workout

Players: One to 25
Equipment: Seven cones, stick

Set up the first three cones as you did for the defensive circuit. After the third cone is in place, take the remaining four cones and stagger them, leading from the third cone back to the 25-yard line. If you are standing at the third cone and facing the 25-yard line, place the fourth cone on an angle to the right about six yards from the 50. The fifth cone is angled to the left, six yards from the fourth cone. Continue placing cones in this zigzag fashion until the four cones create a zigzag between the 50 and the 25. The last cone of this zigzag is on the 25-yard line, parallel to the first cone.

With your stick in the shake hands grip, start at the first cone and stride at about 75 percent of your sprinting stride to the second cone. Break down your steps as you approach that cone and fake to the left of the cone. Change your direction to move to the right and sprint down the 50-yard line to the third cone. When you sprint, hold your stick in just your right hand. Break down your steps as you approach the third cone and return your stick to the shake hands grip. Slow down your speed and change your direction to zigzag to the fourth cone. Continue zigzagging back and forth between the remaining cones using dramatic body fakes. When you get past the seventh cone, jog back to the starting cone and repeat.

Keep Your Balance

Players: One
Equipment: Stick, stopwatch or timer

This drill is a timed running exercise in which you move in a clockwise direction using the stroke line as the center of the circle. Start on the penalty stroke line with two hands on your stick in the shake hands grip. When the clock starts, sprint to the left post of the goal, touching the post with one hand. Quickly turn and sprint back to the penalty stroke and touch the stroke line with one hand. Pivot and sprint to the right goalpost and touch the post. Turn and sprint back to the penalty stroke and touch the stroke line. Turn again and sprint parallel to the end line until you reach the circle line. Touch the line with one hand, pivot, and sprint back to the penalty stroke line. Turn another 90 degrees and sprint away from the cage until you reach the top of the circle line; touch the line with one hand, pivot, and sprint back to the penalty stroke line. Turn 90 degrees and run parallel to the end line in the opposite direction. Touch the circle line, pivot, and return to the stroke line. When you are sprinting, hold your stick in both hands in the shake hands grip. When you reach out to touch the line, take one hand off the stick.

Air Dribble

Players: One
Equipment: Stick and ball

Hold your stick parallel to the ground at your waist with the flat side of the stick facing the sky. With two hands on the stick, tuck the handle and your left hand along your left waist with your left elbow pointing out. Your right hand is near the bottom of the stick on the shaft. Place the ball on the flat toe of the stick, balancing it there. Throw the ball up in the air and continue hitting it with the flat side of the stick to keep it up in the air. This is air dribbling. Count how many dribbles you can complete before losing control of the ball. This is a fun game that will improve your hand-eye coordination and increase your level of comfort with the stick and ball. As you become more comfortable with this, try hitting the ball up with different parts of the stick—the inside edge, the outside edge, the top of the handle. In addition, when you feel more comfortable, instead of starting by placing the ball on the toe of your stick, scoop the ball straight up off the ground and begin your air dribbles from there. Have fun with this.

3

DRIBBLING

No matter the sport, there is nothing more exciting than a player stealing the ball from the other team and sprinting down the field or court on a fast breakaway. The sudden change of pace thrills spectators and players alike. In order to be such a crowd pleaser in field hockey, you must learn how to dribble the ball.

WHAT IS DRIBBLING?

As defined in *Webster's Collegiate Dictionary*, 10th edition, to dribble is "to propel by successive slight taps or bounces with hand, foot, or stick." Just as in soccer, dribbling in field hockey is when one player runs with the ball down the field to gain ground. Regardless of your position on the field, dribbling is a required skill. You use it to move into a space, escape from pressure, set up a pass or shot, or to dodge an opponent. Every player dribbles the ball to dodge around the opponent and move into a space. There are

Dribbling is an individual skill used to advance the ball, escape danger, create space, and take on a defender. It is a basic element of field hockey.

33

different dribbling techniques to use depending on what kind of situation you're in on the field. Mastering them all will assist you in becoming a complete player.

Controlled Dribbling

The controlled dribble, or tight dribble, is used to maneuver the ball through tight spaces. At some point in every game, you'll have to rely on controlled dribbling. Midfielders use controlled dribbling most often because the middle of the field is a high-traffic area.

Stand in the offensive position and hold the stick in the shake hands grip. Drop your right hand lower on the stick for greater ball control. Shift your stick so the flat surface faces forward and the toe is off to the right of your body. Bend your knees until the toe of your stick touches the ground. Place the ball in front of the flat surface of the toe. Bend your elbows away from your body. Keep the ball in front of your feet and to the right of your body at a comfortable dribbling distance.

Push the ball forward with the stick, moving your body forward to stay with the ball. Begin with walking steps and tap the ball ahead of you as you go. Stay low to the ground with your knees bent. It's important to stay balanced as you dribble. It enables you to change direction, slow down, or stop. To maintain balance, stick out your rear end as if you're about to sit down, so your knees don't extend beyond your toes. This positioning keeps your center of gravity low and automatically causes your posture to straighten. Keep your head up to see everything that is happening on the field. When you dribble keep your eyes on the ball but your head facing straight ahead so you can easily glance around to see where the other players are. As UNC's coach Shelton says, "Be aggressive and smart, get your head up, and have good vision."

After you walk around the field and are comfortable with

With your knees bent and upper body leaning forward, keep the ball out in front of you to dribble. This allows you to accelerate with the ball without having it get trapped under your feet.

the dribbling position, increase the speed of your dribble. Run forward as you dribble, keeping your body low and the ball in front of you.

Every now and then glance up to practice dribbling with your eyes off the ball. Too often beginners in the sport are looking straight down at their feet and the ball and they forget to look up. You'll never be able to dodge the opponent or pass to a teammate if you can't see them!

THE RIGHT DIRECTION

A natural dribbling strategy against the defense is to dribble on a forward diagonal to the right of the defender. By moving to the right on a diagonal, you are naturally moving to the defender's nonstick side, making it difficult for her to defend against you. The ball is off to your right side and the defender is off to your left. She is forced to use her reverse stick to defend against you, or she has to get her feet around to get on her strong stick side. This takes precious time and allows you to burst past her into space.

To pass to the right from a dribble, pedal your feet out to the left of the ball and square your shoulders to your passing target. Send a strong pass to your teammate.

Passing to the left side is much easier because your body and stick are naturally positioned to execute a pass to the left. Simply move the ball so it is in front of your lead foot and hit the ball to your teammate. To drive the ball to your teammate, slide your right hand up so it is next to your left, cock your wrists back, and strike the ball with authority.

On grass, continuously tap, or slightly jab, the ball to move it forward. Keep your stick in a vertical position with the toe on the ground. If you're having a hard time controlling the ball, drop your right hand lower on the stick. This increases your control of the

This position is often referred to as the "triple threat" position. The attacker is able to dribble, pass, or shoot from this stance.

When you have open space in front of you, push the ball farther out in front of you to increase your dribbling speed. Push the ball a few yards out in front and sprint onto it.

stick. Less effort is needed to dribble on artificial surfaces because the ball glides in front of the stick with no resistance to the forward movement. Simply touching the ball with your stick provides enough energy to keep the ball moving with you.

Speed Dribbling

Speed dribbling is also sometimes called loose dribbling because the ball is not tight on your stick. Use it when you have open space in front of you (like a breakout, for example). In this move, dribble the ball while sprinting at top speed. Your body positioning is identical to the controlled dribble. Keep the ball in front of you and dribble it off your right side, so you can sprint down the field at top speed without tripping over it.

Because you're traveling at top speed, tap the ball about one foot ahead of your stick as you run. Continue dribbling the ball at this distance until the open space closes up or a defensive player approaches. This is not a dribble to use when players are in close proximity. With the ball coming off your stick, the defense will easily knock it out of your possession. It is imperative that you are smart with your speed dribble and use it only when no one else is around.

TAKE IT TO THE TURF

On artificial surfaces, a speed dribble is a full-on sprint with the stick pushing the ball from behind. Use the speed dribble to travel down either sideline—the sideline provides extra protection against the defense. On turf, the speed dribble is executed with one hand. On a fast breakaway, a one-handed dribbling move allows you to sprint faster because you can use your second arm to pump while you run.

On the right side, hold the stick at the top of the handle in your right hand. The **V** formed by your right thumb and pointer finger is centered down the middle of the flat side of the stick. Angle the flat side of the stick toward the sky so the bottom edge of the toe is underneath the lower half of the ball. Keep the ball out in front of you and off to the right side of your body. Push the ball forward as you sprint down the field.

On the left side of the field, hold the stick in your left hand. Hold the stick at the top of the handle in the reverse grip position with the toe of the stick pointing in toward you and the flat face angled toward the sky. Dribble along the left sideline and keep the ball in front of you and to the left of your body. Place the edge of the toe underneath the lower half of the ball and push the ball forward using your right arm to pump while you sprint.

Indian Dribbling

You are already familiar with Indian dribbling from chapter 2, Understanding the Basics. In the exercise at the end of that chapter, you learned to Indian dribble by standing in place and moving the ball up and back the length of a stick laid on the ground in front of you. Remember that drill when Indian dribbling. Use the forehand and reverse grips to move the ball.

To Indian dribble, push and pull the ball back and forth in front of you. Mastering this advanced dribbling technique will make you difficult to defend.

Indian dribbling on the run is the same basic movement except you are moving forward, so the pushes and pulls move at 45° angles forward. It's a more difficult form of dribbling to execute, but it's also more difficult for the opponent to defend. Use the Indian dribble when moving through crowded areas on the field. Its quick ball movement does not allow enough time for the defense to get their stick on the ball.

To become comfortable with Indian dribbling, begin by dribbling in place. Stand in an offensive attack stance with your knees bent, weight centered, and head over the ball. Start with the ball in front of your right foot and use your forehand dribbling grip to push it over toward your left foot. Shift to the reverse grip and pull the ball back to its starting position. Continue this movement—back and forth, back and forth. As you become more comfortable, move forward with the ball. The Indian dribble pulls are no longer straight back and forth in front of your feet, but instead are on a diagonal forward. Pull the ball in front of the foot that you are stepping on. Start with smaller steps and work your way up, ending with a run.

BODY LANGUAGE

Body language is just as important as stick control when you are dribbling through traffic. Body fakes and deceptive footwork are extremely useful when dribbling in tight spaces. Review chapter 2, Understanding the Basics, for a refresher in body fakes, changing speed, and changing direction. When you have the ball—for that moment—you're in control of the game. It is your job to keep the ball in your team's possession. This is accomplished by smart dribbling or passing to open teammates. Body language plays a critical role in maintaining possession.

Coach Shelton says that in the United States, offensive hockey players don't use enough deception in their game. You must be confident in your movements. Control the defense. Make them commit to you and then blow past them. Incorporate deceptive body language and footwork in your dribbling technique so that it becomes second nature.

DODGES

As you move the ball down the field, you will encounter defenders throwing themselves and their sticks in front of you in an attempt to get the ball. So how do you avoid this? Dodge them. What type of dodge you decide to use will be determined by where the defender is positioned. There are many different dodges you can use to evade a defender: pull back, pull right, pull left, spin right, spin left, and a small scoop over the opponent's stick. Every dodge is accompanied by a body fake and quick footwork. The more realistic your body fakes, the more likely you are to fool your opponent and slip past her untouched. Remember, as the dribbler, only you know what you are going to do with the ball. This is a huge advantage. Use your body fakes and footwork to manipulate the defense.

Pulling Back

The pull back is a simple way to create more space for yourself. As you dribble, break down your steps. Turn the stick to the reverse position with your left hand, but keep the stick to the right of your body. The toe points toward you and the flat side is in front of the ball rather than pushing it from behind. Use the stick as a brake to stop the ball from moving forward. Time your breakdown so your feet and the ball stop at the same time. Lead with your left foot and keep the ball on your right side.

Take a step back by pushing off your left foot and onto your right foot. As you do this, pull the ball back with you, using the reverse side of the stick. Pull hard and check the ball by quickly moving your stick behind the ball in the forehand shake hands grip. Repeat until you have the room you need to look around the field for a pass. Never pull the ball back farther than where you are stepping. If the ball goes behind you, it is out of your possession and in an area where the opponent can get to it.

Pulling Right

The most common dodge is the pull right. In this dodge, pull the ball to your right and move around the defender on her nonstick side. This dodge is executed from a controlled dribble when you approach a defender head on.

The goal with any dodge is to make the defender commit to you. Make her think she is going to get the ball—and then pull it away from her at the last second. With this in mind, dribble close enough to her to make her think she has a chance at the ball.

As you close in, dribble on a diagonal to your left, the defender's stick side. Dribble hard so it's believable, thus making the defender commit to her right. With your head over the ball, step hard onto your left foot and move the ball as if you are going to continue around her to the left. Use an upper body fake toward the left, and at the last minute push off the outside of your left foot and step on a slight diagonal back and to the right. Shift your hands to the reverse stick position and use the reverse stick to pull the ball to the right, keeping it in front of your right foot. Your pull is just out of reach of the defender. Once you pull the ball to the right, catch it with your forehand shake hands grip in front of your right foot and quickly explode to the right of the defender, passing her on her nonstick side. Practice the movement slowly at first before working on speed. Once you understand the mechanics of the move, increase your speed.

Pulling Left

Pulling to the left requires a quick stick and quick feet—more so than any other dodge. This dodge is also executed from a controlled dribble as you approach the defender. Dribble on a diagonal to the right of the defender, moving the ball to her nonstick side.

Like any dodge, the purpose is to make her commit to you just before you pull the ball to an open space. To do this, dribble close enough to her to make her think she has a chance at getting the ball. When she commits, step hard on your right foot and pump your head and upper body to the right. Immediately push off the outside of your right foot and step slightly back and to the left. As you

As you approach the defender, slow down and get your body under control (above). In order to accelerate, you have to be traveling at less than full speed. Step hard to the left (opposite page, top) and lean forward with your upper body (or feint). This shifts the defender's weight in that direction. Quickly switch to the reverse grip and pull the ball back across to the right. Accelerate to the right past the defender with the ball (opposite page, bottom).

step, pull the ball in the same direction, keeping it in front of your left foot.

Catch the ball with your reverse stick to keep it in your control and quickly move your feet around so you are behind the ball. Wheel your feet around to the outside of the ball and explode off your back foot around the opponent. Practice the movement slowly to understand what your stick and feet are doing before working up to game speed. Once you feel comfortable with the movement of the stick and ball, try the move in the game. The only way to measure the quality of your move is to incorporate it into competition.

SECRET TO SUCCESS

When executing either a left or right pull, always pull the ball hard and strong. A weak pull is easily intercepted by the defense. Execute all your offensive moves with authority and strength. Pull the ball about one stick length. Catch the ball with your stick at the end of your pull to stop it from flying out of your control.

Spin to the Right

The right spin move is an advanced dodge that is executed from the straight dribble position. As you approach the defender, dribble on a diagonal to the left as you would when setting up for a pull to the right. Dribble to her stick side and plant your right foot just outside and slightly ahead of her right foot. Keep your weight on the balls of your feet and the ball in front of your left foot. The back of your right shoulder faces the defender's right shoulder and your body blocks her from the ball as you spin.

As soon as you plant your right foot, pivot away from the defender (counterclockwise) and swing your left foot around so your back is to your opponent and your hips are open and facing your defensive end. Your left foot crosses in front of the defender and is planted in front of her left foot. Next, pivot on your left foot and swing your right foot around so that you are now facing forward again, but on the nonstick side of your opponent—the opposite side that you initially dribbled toward. It is essential that you keep your movements fluid and the ball moving when spinning. If you stop moving your feet and the ball and simply stand with your back to the opponent and your body protecting the ball, a penalty will be called for obstructing the defender from the ball.

While your body is doing all this spinning, keep two hands on the stick in a strong shake hands grip. Pull the ball with the forehand toe of the stick in the direction of your left foot as it drops back and swings around to the right side. In other words, the ball trails the path of the left foot. Drop your right shoulder and bend your right elbow to get the stick behind the ball as it spins with your body. In this spin move, the left hand is leading the stick in the direction of the spin, but the right hand provides the power. Your right foot follows closely behind the ball.

Spinning Left

The left spin move requires skillful use of the reverse stick, but is a lot of fun to execute. The best way to describe the spin move is to simply reverse everything you did for the right spin move.

Dribble on a diagonal to the right, moving to your opponent's nonstick side. As you approach her, plant your left foot on the outside of her left foot. Keep your weight on the ball of your left foot and pivot away from her toward your defensive end of the field (clockwise). Shift to the reverse grip and hold your stick so the flat side is in front of the ball and the toe is pointing toward you. Swing your right foot around, opening your hips up to the back of the field. Plant your right foot in front of your opponent's right foot. Pull the ball with the reverse stick in the direction of your spin. Your left foot follows the ball as you pivot on your right foot. Continue using the reverse stick until you complete the spin and come out on the opposite side of the opponent. Bend your elbows and drop your shoulders to the ground so you can get your weight behind the ball and really push it as you spin. Keep the ball tight on your stick and your stick on the ground to make sure the opponent cannot intercept the ball. Complete the spin by bringing your left foot around so it is next to your right foot.

Once you've beaten a defender, quickly slide behind her to cut her off. This makes it much more difficult for her to recover.

You can either continue spinning and use the reverse stick to cut behind the opponent, making sure that she won't be able to interfere with your play, or you can get your feet around and use the strong forehand grip to continue moving forward. If you spin successfully, you will have enough time to get your feet around and move forward. At times you will find that the reverse stick is quicker and easier to use against a fast defense. Explode forward past your defender on her strong stick side.

Small Scoop

Another excellent dodge is a small scoop over the defender's stick. A good time to use the scoop dodge is when a defender has her stick on the ground in your dribbling path. As you dribble to her, break down your steps, slow the ball, and control your stick. Drop your right shoulder and lower your left hand so the stick is angled back with the

The small scoop is especially effective when a defender attempts to use a horizontal block tackle.

face of the stick toward the sky. The bottom of the toe of the stick is under the lower half of the ball. Lift the ball over the defender's stick in a small scoop. Elevate the ball high enough to clear the defender's stick, but not so high that you risk losing possession. Move with the ball over the defender's stick and past the defender.

DRILLS AND GAMES

Working the Ball

Players: One
Equipment: Stick, ball, five cones
Distance: 25 yards

Line up five cones five yards apart from each other. Start five yards away from the first cone and dribble through the cones without using your reverse stick. Move to the left of the first cone and pass it and then to the right of the second cone. Continue weaving through the cones until you reach the end of the line. When you move to the left of the cones, get your feet around and drop your left elbow closer to the ground. This opens up the flat side of the stick to direct the ball around the cone while maintaining your forehand grip position. Do this five complete times up and back. After five times, weave through the cones using the reverse stick. When you move to the left of the cone, shift to a reverse grip and pull the ball with the reverse stick. Go up and back five times again.

Shifting Gears

Players: At least two
Equipment: Stick and ball, whistle
Distance: 50 yards

One player is on the end line with a stick and ball. One player or the coach is in the middle of the field with a whistle. At the first whistle, the dribbler moves the ball forward in a controlled dribble. When the player or coach in the middle of the field blows the whistle again, the dribbler quickly pulls the ball back and then explodes forward in a speed dribble. The next time the whistle is blown, the dribbler breaks down her steps and slows down to a controlled dribble.

This series is repeated until the dribbler reaches the 50-yard line. The whistler can blow her whistle as few or as many times as she likes, however the dribbler should have at least three pull-back-and-explode series during her run to the 50. Repeat this twice and then switch places.

Keep Your Head Up

Players: At least two
Equipment: Stick and ball
Distance: 25 yards

All players line up on the 50-yard line. One player or coach (without a stick or ball) is 20 yards in front of and facing the group. At her command, the players on the 50 dribble forward but keep their eyes on the coach. The coach tells the group which way to dribble by pointing with her arm to the left, right, forward, or backward. Dribblers move with their balls in the direction the coach's arm is pointing. Because they are facing each other, if the coach is pointing left, the dribbler is pulling right. If the coach is pointing forward toward the dribbler, the dribbler is pulling the ball back. Dribblers must keep their heads up to see what direction to dribble. There is no talking in this drill.

Queen of the Circle

Players: The whole team
Equipment: Stick and ball
Distance: The circle

All players go into the circle with a stick and a ball (each player has a ball). Each player Indian dribbles around the circle, working on stick and ball control.

You cannot leave the circle. Keep your head up and watch your ball and your teammates as they dribble. When the ball comes off a teammate's stick or when you see a teammate who's not protecting the ball, take your stick off your own ball and jab at hers to knock it out of the circle. By sending a teammate's ball out of the circle, you eliminate her from the game. As soon as her ball crosses out of the circle, she's done.

When you move to knock someone else's ball out of the circle, keep an eye on your own ball—another teammate could be hitting yours out of the circle while you're working on someone else. Trust no one! The last player remaining in the circle with her ball wins.

Dodges

Players: One
Equipment: Five cones, stick and ball
Distance: 35 yards

Set up five cones seven yards away from each other in a straight line. These cones are the defenders. Start five yards away from the fist cone. Control dribble to the first cone. As you approach, dribble to the left and pull right in front of the cone as if it was a defender. Pull right and explode past the cone (defender) and slow down to a controlled dribble again. When you approach the second cone, dribble on a diagonal to the right and pull left in front of the cone (defender). Explode past the defender to the left.

At the third cone, dribble on a diagonal to the left and spin right around the cone. Dribble on a diagonal to the right at the fourth cone and spin to the left around it. At the last cone, pull back and scoop the ball over the top of the cone. Go up and back the line of cones, or defenders, four times.

To increase difficulty, replace the cones with teammates. The teammates are dummy defenders. Although they are not attempting to take the ball from you, they are standing with their sticks on the ground. This gives you a better idea of the reaching area of the defense and how hard and far you should pull the ball.

4
PASSING AND RECEIVING

Coaches constantly stress the importance of teamwork. How many times have you heard the expression, "There is no 'I' in the word 'team'"? It is true that certain individuals possess superior skill, but even talented players must learn to work within the framework of the team. A winning team boasts a group of players who complement one another. This philosophy rings true in all team sports: You must blend your skills with the skills of your teammates to become a complete player and to create a winning environment.

To use your teammates (and allow them to use you), you must become adept in two essential areas of the game: passing and receiving. Passing is the quickest, most effective method of advancing the ball. Passing stops the opponent from double-teaming an offensive player; it allows you to attack using the length and width of the field; and you can catch defensive players off guard and out of position. Passing creates space, forces the defense to constantly readjust, and creates scoring opportunities. Most important, passing the ball gets you from Point A to Point B much faster than dribbling. Have someone time you with a stopwatch as you dribble the ball 35 yards. Then, record the time it takes to pass the ball 35 yards. This simple experiment clearly illustrates that distance is covered much quicker when the ball is passed rather than dribbled. You simply cannot outrun the ball.

That said, a great pass is only as good as a player's ability to receive the ball. If a teammate feeds you a beautiful pass to your stick and you're unable to receive and control the ball, the pass is wasted. You must develop "touch" when receiving the ball. In other words, you

Many goals are the result of a series of great passes and controlled receptions.

have to learn to keep the ball close to your stick. If the ball jumps off your stick, you'll lose possession and your team loses an opportunity.

There are many different types of passes, but the effectiveness of each type is determined by accuracy and timing. If either of these two elements is missing from your passes, the effort will be fruitless.

PASSING GROUND BALLS

Depending on the game situation, you may make a pass on the ground or in the air. Whenever possible, pass the ball on the ground. Roll is much easier to judge than flight, and it's much easier to receive a pass on the ground than one that travels through the air. In order to receive a ball out of the air, your teammate is forced to raise her stick, which will frequently entice a dangerous play call from the referee.

Imagine passing a sponge ball to a three-year-old. If you roll it along the ground, she'll have a much greater chance of stopping the ball as opposed to snagging it out of the air. Passing the ball in the air raises the level of hand-eye coordination required to control the ball. The same idea applies in field hockey. Trapping a pass rolling along the ground simplifies things for the receiver. Always keep things as simple as possible.

There are three basic methods of passing the ball along the ground: push passing, reverse push passing, and hitting. Each method requires its own special technique. To be a complete player, you must perfect all three passes. You'll certainly need to use all three in competition.

STICK TIPS

Accuracy and timing are critical when making passes, but there are other factors to consider when distributing the ball. Listed below are a few steadfast rules.

1. Make sure your teammate is open before passing her the ball.
2. Always have a clear passing lane to your intended target.
3. Accuracy is absolutely critical on short passes. Longer passes permit some margin for error.
4. Try to time your pass so that your teammate doesn't break stride. Her running speed dictates the pace of your pass and your aiming point.
5. Know the surface you're playing on. Wet grass, burnt grass, high grass, low grass, artificial surface—all will affect the pace of your passes.
6. Remember, think "pass" first, "dribble" second.

Push Passes

A push pass is primarily used for passes that are five to 15 yards in distance. It's the most commonly used pass in field hockey, so it's important to swiftly master the technique and practice it every day. Push passes are easy to control and can be executed quickly. They are easy to command in direction and pace. The first order of business is to develop a quick release with accurate results. Then, work on adjusting the pace of your passes.

Quick, accurate passes greatly depend on balance. The correct positioning of your feet and lower body—your base—help you achieve balance.

To begin, get into the athletic position. The athletic position is a standard setup used by athletes in many sports. Picture a tennis player awaiting a serve, a goalkeeper poised for a shot on goal, or a basketball player guarding her opponent. They're all in a balanced position ready for an explosive movement in any direction. Spread your feet slightly farther than shoulder width apart. Flex your knees and bend slightly forward at the waist. Your weight should be balanced in the middle.

To execute a push pass, point your left shoulder at the target, using the shake hands grip on your stick. Lower your upper body to the ball so the end of your stick rests against the lower half of the ball. Keeping the stick against the ball disguises the timing and direction of your pass.

The ball is positioned in your control box area, toward your rear foot. Because there is no backswing in a push pass, you need to move the ball back a bit so you can get some momentum going into your forward swing. Hold the face of your stick at a slightly closed angle to make sure the ball stays on the ground.

To begin your forward swing, start by shifting your weight forward onto your front leg. Bend your front knee forward to the target. As you do this, your upper body moves a few inches forward. Keep the stick against the ball during this movement and cock your hands back slightly. This allows you to generate more power with your forward swing. When executing a push pass, your rear arm (the hand lower on the stick) supplies the power while the lead arm controls the direction of the stick.

As you're making your forward swing, transfer your weight forward onto, and then out over, your front leg. This transfer of energy supplies additional force for a crisp pass.

Keep your head down on the ball throughout the swing. Do not lift your head prematurely to catch a glimpse of your pass. Your friends can tell you all about it after the game.

Once the ball is released, it's very important to follow through down the target line. If you don't follow through, your distance control and direction suffer. Extend your lead arm to the target in your follow-through, so your stick is pointing at the target when you complete the pass.

A push pass is the most common method of passing the ball. It's the quickest and most accurate form of distributing the ball.

Your stick points to the intended target as you follow through.

The push pass technique can also be used when shooting on goal from close range. The quick release time can catch goalkeepers off guard. Also, because there is no indication during the setup in which direction your shot will travel, it's extremely difficult for goalies to anticipate your shots.

STRIKING GOLD

Women's field hockey was introduced as an Olympic sport in 1980. The games that year were held in the Soviet Union, and 35 nations (including the United States) boycotted the Olympics in protest of the Soviet invasion of Afghanistan. Five of the six nations scheduled to compete in the inaugural women's field hockey tournament were among those who boycotted the games.

The Moscow organizing committee and the International Olympic Committee scrambled to find replacements. They contacted Zimbabwe to join the games just five weeks before competition. The Zimbabwe team was not selected until the weekend before the Olympics. Much to everyone's disbelief, Zimbabwe remained undefeated through the tournament and won the gold medal.

Reverse Push Passes

A reverse push pass is more difficult to execute because it requires unfamiliar positioning of the hands and feet, but it's an effective form of passing when you don't have time to set up for a normal push pass. You won't be able to send the ball great distances using the reverse push pass method, so use it only for short passes.

The setup is similar to a push pass, only everything is reversed. Your right foot is now your front foot, and the left foot is the rear foot. Use the reverse grip and point your right shoulder at the target. Position the ball in your control box area and closer to your rear foot. Close the face of the stick slightly and rest it against the lower half of the ball. Press your hands forward and keep your weight on your rear foot and your head centered over the ball. As you make your pass, transfer your weight forward, onto, and out over your front foot. Your left hand pulls the stick as your right hand pushes through the lower half of the ball. The right hand supplies most of the power for this pass. Follow through completely by extending your arms toward the target.

This pass is comparable to kicking a soccer ball with your opposite foot or executing an opposite-hand layup in basketball. It's a skill that doesn't always come naturally and must be practiced over and over. The reverse push pass may be used sparingly, but it's a very helpful tool when you're in a crunch. Don't view it as a weakness and ignore it. Practice it every day and you'll improve as a player.

Step with your right foot to initiate the reverse push pass (above). Push with your right hand and pull the stick with your left hand (above, next page).

Hitting

Imagine you're playing in a game and the ball is in your defensive end. Your opponent turns the ball over to you and you look up and see one of your teammates streaking 20 yards downfield. She has her defender beat by five yards and, if given the ball, has a legitimate scoring chance. A reverse push pass would never reach her. A forward push pass might reach her but by the time the ball gets there, the defender will have caught up to her mark. In order to take advantage of the opportunity, you've got to send her a hit.

Players use the hit, or "drive" as it is sometimes called, to move the ball quickly over long distances. You take a backswing and swing the stick at the ball, generating significant force at and through impact.

Hitting is not simply confined to long passes. You can use it for short passes that must arrive at your intended target quickly. Say, for example, your teammate makes a sharp cut and is open only for a brief instant. You've got to get the ball to her immediately to advance play.

Hitting is also often used for shooting. Hard-hit balls allow the goalkeeper less time to react and make a save. The hitting stroke has many similarities to swings used in other sports such as golf and baseball. You align your body sideways to the ball (shoulders are parallel to the target line), take a backswing, transfer your weight forward, rotate the hips and hit through the ball. One difference with the field hockey swing is that the rules do not allow the stick to travel above the shoulders during the follow-through. This restriction forces you to inhibit

Defensive players often hit the ball out of the backfield to clear the ball out of danger and to the side.

your hip rotation and use a greater lateral weight shift. Bend your front leg and allow your weight to transfer outside your front leg. This keeps the follow-through of the stick down the target line and below the shoulders. If you were to stiffen your front leg, as is done in both the baseball and golf swing, your hips would fully rotate and the stick would travel up and off the target line.

Hitting occurs when you're stationary or on the run, depending on the game situation. To review the mechanics, let's assume you're at rest. Position the ball in line with your rear foot approximately six to nine inches out away from your body. (The exact distance depends on your height and length of arms.) Use the shake hands grip, but with a slight variation. Bring both hands together like a softball player grips her bat. Grip the stick near the end of the handle for maximum power, or choke down a few inches for greater control. Remember, it's good to have a firm grip, but don't squeeze the handle too tightly. This allows tension to creep into your grip, and tension will diminish accuracy and decrease your swing speed.

From the athletic position, bend at the waist as if you were starting to touch to your toes. Once the face of your stick is flush with the ball on the ground, you're in position to begin your backswing. Bring the stick straight back with two hands. Coil your front knee inward as your weight shifts back to the inside of your rear leg. Keep your upper body over the ball with your head down. Bend your lead arm at the elbow during the backswing as your rear arm simply folds in along your side. As your hands reach waist level, cock your wrists so the stick points upward to the sky behind you. Think of the stick as the arm of a clock: it should point to approximately 10:00.

The forward swing is initiated by pulling the front hip forward. Shift your weight forward onto your front leg by pushing off your rear foot. Pull the stick down and forward to the ball with your lead arm. The rear arm simply takes a free ride until a few inches before contact. At that point, fire the face of the stick toward the ball by snapping your wrists forward to and through the ball. This adds force to your hits. At the point of contact, the flat face of your stick is at a right angle and your hands are both pointing straight down at the ball. Keep your head down as you strike the lower half of the ball.

During the forward swing, establish tempo by executing a fluid, rhythmic swing. Do not try to kill it. Coaches often say "less is more," meaning the less effort, the greater distance and velocity of your hits. If you try to swing too hard, you'll diminish the speed of your swing, which *decreases* the distance and velocity of your hits. Stay relaxed.

As with the push pass, continue to follow your shot down the target line after contact. This extension is critical, because as the top hand fires the face of the stick at the ball, players often make the mistake of rolling their hand over prematurely, sort of slapping at the ball instead of driving through it. The stick will point to the left of your target just after contact, as opposed to correctly pointing *at* the target.

Make sure you keep your head over the ball and transfer your weight forward onto your front foot when hitting the ball. The tendency for beginners is to allow the front shoulder to lift up prematurely. The face of the stick will then dip down and undercut the ball. This results in balls being hit uncontrollably through the air. Also, by

To send a long pass, slide your right hand up on the stick to bring your hands together. Take a longer backswing and use your wrists to fire the face of the stick to the ball.

lifting the front shoulder and head up, your weight never fully transfers onto your front leg. This sacrifices power, reducing the velocity and length of your hits.

STICK TIPS

Players make more mistakes with hitting than with any other type of pass. Because the backswing and downswing are so powerful, there is a greater likelihood of error. Here are some common mistakes to watch for when driving the ball.

- *Failing to align your feet and lower body to the target.* If you're not aligned correctly to the target, you'll be less accurate. To compensate for poor alignment, players often attempt to manipulate the face of the stick with their hands when striking the ball. This causes mishits or hits stroked with less force.
- *Shifting your weight too far, too soon.* Weight shift is essential for executing a strong hit, but if you transfer your weight too far ahead (of your swing), you'll lose power. Your hands will get ahead of the ball and the face of the stick will drag behind. In addition, you'll be unable to generate any hip rotation, which results in diminished power.
- *Coming up out of your swing prematurely.* When your front shoulder raises up before contact, the face of your stick will raise up as well. Your stick will catch the top half of the ball and produce a weak hit. Stay down and through the ball when driving it.
- *Undercutting the ball.* Hitting too far beneath the ball will cause the ball to fly up in the air. Any hit that flies above the knees is considered a dangerous hit, and you'll receive a penalty. Hit the lower half of the ball, but don't dig underneath it.
- *High stick violation.* You can be guilty of a high stick violation in both the backswing and the follow-through. Keep the stick below your shoulders, especially when hitting with other players in close proximity.

PASSING AERIAL BALLS

It's easier to pass the ball along the ground, but there are situations that require you to loft the ball in the air. The most obvious reason for an aerial pass is that a player or stick is blocking your passing lane. If your teammate is open, you've got to deliver the goods in any manner that the rules permit. If an aerial pass is the only way to get her the ball, then serve it up.

Air travel is also the quickest and most reliable route for a ball when using a push pass. The ball encounters very little friction (only wind resistance) when traveling through the air. Wet or high grass slows the ball down, and a choppy surface can adversely affect the direction of a pass. Field hockey is a fast game, and a slow or unpredictable roll can ruin an offensive attack or defensive clearing. There are no bad hops in the sky.

The Flick Pass

Hits or drives often lift the ball in the air, but to make a short and precise aerial pass, flick the ball. The most important use of the flick is in penalty strokes or shooting the ball with power, but for this chapter, we'll only discuss passing. The flick pass is a very useful tool on offense and defense, and like many other components of the game, takes practice to perfect.

Similar to the push pass, flicks are made without a backswing. The face of the stick rests on the ball during the setup. In this case, however, the bottom edge of the stick face digs *under* the backside of the ball. (When playing a push pass, the face leans against the bottom half of the ball.) To accomplish this, lower your right shoulder and position the ball ahead of your front foot.

Lower your right shoulder and angle the face of the stick slightly back so to dig under the ball. Most important, position the ball in front of your left foot.

Push the stick forward and upward to lift the ball into the air. The length of your follow-through dictates the distance of your flick.

To lift the ball in the air, adjust the path of your forward swing. As you shift your weight to your front leg, fire the stick sharply upward and forward. Your right arm exerts greater effort for this type of swing. Imagine tossing a bucket of water underhand onto a flame. This upward, explosive movement will help the ball get airborne. Keep your body low and your head over the ball.

The length of your follow-through dictates the distance of your flick. A short, abbreviated finish produces a short pass. This is for "touch" passes when you simply need to jump a defender's stick to deliver your pass. Your stick face curls up quickly like a fishhook. A long, extended finish increases the distance of your flick pass. Perhaps a defender is 10 yards away and could reach out and block a ground pass, or an offensive attacker is tightly marked and you opt to send her a lead pass that she can run to. A long flick pass will get the job done.

WET, NOT WILD

All major international games are played on wet artificial turf. Before a game, the field is sprayed with a huge water cannon. The water makes the ball hug the ground and keeps the ball from taking funny bounces. The water also keeps the players' shoes from gripping the turf too tightly. This helps prevent twisted knees and other injuries.

The height of your follow-through also controls the height of your pass. If you finish at knee height, your pass will also travel knee high.

For a higher pass, make your follow-through higher, but remember to keep your stick below your shoulders. An aerial pass that travels around or above the shoulders into a crowd of players will draw a penalty.

RECEIVING THE BALL

The great pass is one of the most beautiful sights in field hockey. It's a skill developed by players through experience. The very best players turn it into an art form.

To capitalize on a teammate's great pass, you must refine your receiving skills. Receiving the ball is most commonly referred to as fielding or trapping. Simply stated, it means taking a pass from a teammate or intercepting an opponent's pass. The key to receiving is bringing the ball under control without a rebound. Doing so enables you to maintain possession of the ball and transition into or continue the attack. Lose control of a pass and you risk losing possession.

> "Good receiving mechanics will place the receiver in a multiple-threat position to hold the ball, elude an opponent, pass to a teammate, dribble to free space, or shoot. It is impossible to overemphasize the importance of sound receiving techniques because they are the prelude to ball possession, stickwork, good passing, shooting, and attack tactics."
>
> —Elizabeth Anders, head field hockey coach,
> Old Dominion University

Receiving skills are extremely critical when accepting a pass off a penalty hit.

When receiving the ball, move your left arm downward so the stick shaft is less vertical. This allows for better touch, keeping the ball under control.

Receiving the Ground Pass—Forehand

The first step in receiving a ground pass is anticipation. You must expect the ball to be passed to you. In ice hockey, National Hockey League legend Wayne Gretzky was arguably the greatest player in the history of his sport. Gretzky had spectacular individual skills, but was most revered for his ability to make his teammates better. His vision on the ice was astounding, and his teammates would often say that they had to keep their stick on the ice at all times because they never knew when "The Great One" might find them with an incredible pass. Players who were always prepared reaped the benefits of playing with Gretzky, but those who were caught off guard failed to take advantage of his passes. Always be alert and ready.

Much like passing, you must be in a good position to receive the ball. When a teammate passes you the ball, shift your body so you'll receive the ball on your right side (if you have time). This is the position that feels most natural, and it also prepares you to make a pass or shoot. Ninety percent of your passes and shots will originate from the right side of your body.

To become consistent at receiving balls, prepare yourself in what is known as the "triple-threat stance." You may have heard this term used on the basketball court. The triple-threat stance enables you to pass, dribble, or shoot once you receive the ball. It also puts you in the best possible position to receive a pass.

Spread your feet slightly farther apart than shoulder width, flex the knees, and bend at the waist. Using the shake hands grip, keep your stick on the ground and make sure there is some flex in your elbows. This allows you to have some touch when fielding the ball. If your arms are fully extended, you become too stiff and run the risk of the ball rebounding off your stick.

The essence of receiving lies in allowing the ball to come to your stick, even if you're on the run. Do not stretch out for the ball. As mentioned, your arms will lock stiff, making it difficult to maintain a soft touch. As you receive the ball, move your left arm ahead of your right arm so it aligns with the front knee. This slightly closes the face of the stick so that if there is a rebound, the ball will rebound downward and not upward. If the ball becomes airborne, it becomes much more difficult to control. Also, move your left arm downward so the stick shaft is farther from vertical (around 45 degrees). This broadens your receiving surface marginally, but also allows for better touch.

On contact, your stick should "give" with the ball. Receiving the ball requires sensitivity in your hands, so keep a loose grip. Gripping the stick too tightly creates tension and diminishes touch. Receive the ball likes it's an egg—you don't want it to crack.

Receiving the Ground Pass—Backhand

Backhand receiving is used when there isn't enough time to position yourself to receive the ball on your right side. Instead, you receive the ball on your left side and reverse your grip and body positioning. Using the reverse grip, point your right shoulder along the ball's line of direction. The flat side of the stick faces the ball, while the toe points to your feet.

As you receive the ball, allow your left hand to shift forward to your right knee. This closes the face of the stick to help trap the ball. Although the reverse grip doesn't feel as natural as the shake hands grip, do not allow tension to creep into your hands. Tension is your enemy.

Once you receive the ball, quickly move the ball to your right side and get into the triple-threat position. Attempting to play the ball from the reverse position is difficult; your options are limited.

Receiving Aerial Balls

Not only are aerial passes more difficult to make, they are more difficult to receive. Difficult, but not impossible. In many cases, it's best to simply let the ball drop to the ground. Prepare your body so it's in position to control the ball once it lands. There are times, however, that an aerial pass is moving at a high velocity. If

Quickly adjust to the reverse grip to use the flat side of the stick to receive the ball.

When taking an aerial pass face on, do not raise the stick's head above your waist (left); this is dangerous. Keep the flat side of the stick facing the ball and deflect the ball so it drops down in front of your feet (right).

you allow it to run its course, it will travel past you and possibly find the stick of an opponent. You've got to do what you can to gather the ball and maintain possession. To control this type of pass, use the following method.

You will encounter two types of aerial passes during games. The first is when you're facing the ball in a stationary position, and the second is when you're on the run and moving away from the passer. Each requires a distinct technique. Always keep in mind that your stick must stay below your shoulders.

When facing an aerial pass, lift your left arm up to the height of your left shoulder. Imagine pouring soda out of a can onto the ground in front of you. This is the action taken by your left arm. It puts the stick in a vertical position (pointing downward). Your right arm simply goes along for the ride. Use the right arm only to make sure the flat side of the stick is facing the incoming pass. As a checkpoint, your right elbow should be held in front of your midsection with the back of the elbow facing behind you.

Flex at the knees as you keep your eyes locked on the ball. As it approaches, adjust the positioning of your stick so the shaft and head are facing the ball. Try to intercept the ball at a level below your midsection. It's easier to handle balls in that area. Let the ball hit your stick below your right hand and have it drop down to the ground below you. Quickly move into triple-threat position.

When you're running away from the source of an aerial pass, look over your shoulder on the side the ball is approaching. Lay your stick out horizontally so you catch the ball on your forehand or reverse grip. Try to drop the ball to the ground a yard or two ahead of you so you can maintain your stride. Angle the flat side of the stick toward the ground so that upon contact the ball is sure to deflect down and not up into the air.

STICK TRIVIA

Field hockey is India's international sport. The men's field hockey team has won eight Olympic gold medals since 1924, the last coming in 1980. In fact, the city of Jalandhar is home to 127 stick manufacturers.

DRILLS AND GAMES

Rapid Fire Push Passing

Players: Four
Equipment: Stick, ball, four cones
Distance: 12 yards

Set up a miniature field that is 12 yards in length. Each end of the field has a goal that is three yards wide. (Use a pair of cones for each goal.) Two yards behind each goal is a player set up in the triple-threat position. Each player's partner stands facing them, 5 yards from the cones. Attempt to pass a ball back and forth as rapidly as possible through the cones using the forehand push pass. Receive and control each pass on the forehand side. Award one team a point for each ball passed between the cones. Play for 45 seconds. Compare your point total against the other two-player team.

Basketball Flicks

Players: At least two
Equipment: Stick, 10 balls, an empty bucket
Distance: 10 yards

Stand 10 yards from an empty bucket. Now, try flicking the ball into the bucket. Execute 10 flicks, then allow your teammates their turns. Whoever sinks the most "baskets" is the sharpshooter of the group.

Driver's Ed

Players: Two
Equipment: Stick, ball, 10 cones
Distance: 25 yards

Position yourself 25 yards from a teammate. Now, use 10 cones to create a passing lane between the two of you. Set two cones three yards apart at five-yard intervals between you and your teammate. Execute 20 drives each, keeping track of how many hits travel the entire length of the passing lane. Try for 15 out of 20.

Semicircle Swirl

Players: One
Equipment: Stick, 10 balls, 10 cones
Distance: 12 yards

Place 10 cones in a semicircle, each cone approximately five yards away from the next. The base of the semicircle is about 12 yards long. Stand in the middle of the base of the semicircle with a stack of balls. Using the push pass technique, attempt to hit each cone. Track your results, recording the number of balls you used to hit all of the cones. In subsequent practice sessions, try to better your record.

5
SHOOTING

Ten, nine, . . . the last seconds of a tied game are ticking away. In one final offensive sweep, your team surges into the circle. As the center forward, you're in a position to score. The left wing sends a strong hit directly in front of the cage. Your stick is on the ground, you're in a low attack position, and your feet are moving toward the goal—but you realize the ball is just out of your reach. You cut around your defender and dive after the ball with your stick outstretched, toe on the ground. Your body stretches through the air, and your stick touches the ball just enough to redirect it into the corner of the cage. Three, two, . . . victory is yours!

BEYOND THE SCOREBOARD

Goals build team confidence, and a confident team is a successful one. The center forward is generally a team's lead scorer, however, all positions in the front half of the field (the front line and midfield) are part of the offensive thrust. In fact, a good team will have players in every position (including sweeper) who can sprint down the field on a breakaway and knock the ball into the cage at any given time. Every player should be familiar with and practice scoring situations; you never know when you will be presented with an opportunity to score.

Goal scorers are generally evasive, quick players with an excellent sense of timing and the ability to stay calm under pressure. They are good passers because they understand how to place the ball accurately in a certain spot. When you think about it, a goal is simply a pass over

In simplest terms, you've got to shoot to score.

the end line—but instead of reaching a teammate's stick, you are aiming to hit the empty spot in the cage.

Balance

Balance is the most important part of shooting successfully in the circle. Keep your knees bent and your body low to the ground—the key to balance is a low center of gravity.

When shooting, start with the ball in front of your rear foot and your weight on the ball of your rear foot. Step toward the cage with your lead foot, pointing your toes toward the goal. When you step, transfer all your weight to your front foot. Keep your knees bent, your head over the ball, and finish with a strong follow-through swing. At the completion of your swing, your stick points at the goal.

Coach Northcroft points out that players often have a hard time shooting because their bodies are off balance. "Players tend to fall back instead of bringing their weight through to the front foot. You must keep your weight close to the ground so you have a low center of gravity and are able to transmit your weight forward."

With the ball sitting just in front of your lead foot, draw your stick back and cock your wrists. The weight of your body is centered, knees flexed, bent at the waist with your eyes over the ball. As you take your forward swing, transfer your weight forward onto your front leg and rotate your hips. Keep your head down and your eyes locked on the ball throughout contact.

Shoot the Ball

It is essential that you keep your stick on the ball and shoot as soon as you enter the circle. Very rarely you will be in a one-on-one situation with the goalie. Only in these situations do you have the time and space to dribble into the circle and dodge around the goalie. Otherwise, shoot the ball as soon as you cross the line into the circle. Too often, players hold on to the ball too long in the circle and end up having it knocked away from them by the defense.

The more shots you get on cage, the more chances you have of scoring a goal. Avoid using a big backswing—this only gives the defense an opportunity to take the ball from you. Dribbling around the circle presents the same problem.

To execute a strong shot with little or no backswing from a dribble, change your body position as you enter the circle so you are set to shoot the ball. As you dribble, shift your body so your left foot is leading and your left shoulder points at the goal. Stay low in your dribble stance as you make this transition. Keep the ball off your rear foot and your weight on your rear foot. Step toward the cage with your lead foot and shoot the ball using one of the shots described later in this chapter.

When receiving a pass from a teammate, get your body in shooting position before the ball gets to you. Establish a lead foot, bend your

Notice how the shooter steps with her lead foot (above). The alignment of her feet shows that she's aiming for the right corner of the cage (below).

Just before contact, the bottom of her foot lifts up off the ground, displaying her forward weight transfer (above). Even after the ball is struck, her upper body stays over the top of the ball as she follows through (below).

knees, stay balanced and low to the ground, and point your shoulder toward the goal. Your lead foot and shoulder are opposite where the ball is coming from, so if the ball is on your right side, your left foot and shoulder are leading. Receive the ball off your back foot with your weight on your back foot. As you receive it, step toward the cage with your front foot and shoot the ball immediately.

Always keep your eyes on the ball and aim for the corners of the cage. "Players are looking at the goal cage before they actually hit the ball so they're mis-hitting it," says Coach Northcroft. "I don't think shots are taken quick enough, at all levels," she continues. "Players want to make it pretty and put a ribbon on top of it. What it really comes down to is the basics of keeping the ball on your stick in the circle and receiving that ball in a position where you're able to swing right away with a quick short swing or place the ball in the right spot with a push or a lift."

U.S. HISTORY OF SHOOTING RULE CHANGES

Throughout all levels of play—high school, collegiate, or international—a goal can only be scored if the ball is shot in the circle. But this was not always the case in the United States. In 1984 the governing body of college athletics, the NCAA, ruled that goals could be scored from anywhere on the field. The purpose of this rule change was to increase excitement by creating higher-scoring games. In 1990 the NCAA modified the rule, stating that goals could only be scored within the 25-yard offensive area. High school and international teams, however, continued to compete with the original rule of goals shot in the circle.

In 1996 the FIH (Fédération Internationale de Hockey) instituted a "no offsides" mandatory experiment. Previously, a player was offsides if he or she was ahead of the ball and closer to the offensive goal line than any opposing defensive player other than the goalie. The no offsides rule affected all levels of play. The FIH noticed that this rule in itself increased scoring and in 1997 determined that the NCAA should return to the original rule of scoring only within the 16-yard circle.

By instituting the no offsides rule (whose status changed from mandatory experiment to official rule in 1998) and returning to scoring only within the circle, the FIH supported the NCAA's desire for exciting, high-scoring games but also maintained consistency among all levels of play.

Following Your Shot

After you've taken your shot, should you stand there and admire it for its power and pinpoint accuracy? Absolutely not! Get off your horse and follow it up.

Once you've taken your shot, return your stick to the shake hands position with your stick on the ground and follow it up. Run forward and prepare for a rebound. If your shot hits the goalie's pads, the ball is going to come back out into the circle, presenting you with the opportunity to slam the ball into the cage with authority. Read the goalie and anticipate what direction she is going to clear the ball in. As soon as your shot is released, run toward the goal and prepare to block the goalie's delivery.

Always keep your stick on the ground to get the rebound. Keep your knees bent, your feet wider than shoulder width apart, and your arms slightly flexed. Break down your steps as if you were a defensive player approaching an offensive opponent who has the ball.

As you collect the rebound and shoot the ball, pay attention to where the goalie is so you can put the ball in the back of the cage. In terms of eluding the goalie, Northcroft offers one tip: Pull to the right. "Make it easier on yourself as a player and pull to the right around the goalie to her nonstick side."

Follow up on every shot. Gathering a rebound can result in an easy goal.

PAY ATTENTION TO THE PADS

Before the game starts, take time to notice what type of leg pads the opposing goalie is wearing. There are two types of pads a goalie usually wears—foam pads or leather cane kickers. Foam pads are superior because the ball rebounds farther off foam, so the goalie's clears will be harder and stronger. Foam pads also provide the goalie with a wider surface area to block shots. All college goalies wear foam pads. When the goalie is wearing foam, give her at least five yards on her clears to rebound the ball.

In high school, you're more likely to find cane kickers. You can tell by appearance that these don't provide as much protection and the ball is not going to travel as far on rebounds. The ball will settle only a foot or two from the goalie, so be more aggressive on the rebound.

Develop a Knack for Scoring

The art of scoring can be developed only through practice, practice, and more practice. The more scoring scenarios you put yourself in during practice, the greater your chances are of remaining calm in front of the cage during a game. Coach Shelton says, "Practice shooting, and practice a variety of shots—even create new shots. Just work on it and have fun with it." According to Coach Shelton, quick, strong shots come from quick, strong wrists. She notices that players often don't take advantage of the power that is in their wrists. So how does one go about increasing wrist strength when hitting? Practice. Line up as if you're about to hit the ball. Lead with your left foot and point your left shoulder at the goal. Cock your wrists back to the right so the stick is extended behind you, parallel to the ground and perpendicular to your body with the toe pointing up. Your arms are slightly flexed, and your wrists are holding the stick below your waist. As you step into the hit, snap your wrists forward so the face of the stick meets the ball and continue through until the ball is released. The stick should finish extended out in front of you, parallel to the ground and perpendicular to your body with the toe pointing up to the sky. Your wrists turn over after hitting the ball and your right arm crosses in front of your body. Practice this motion over and over again, with and without the ball. By including a powerful wrist snap, all of your shots will be stronger.

Coach Morett agrees that variety is essential. "To be successful shooting the ball you have to have a variety of shooting options. You have to shoot the ball strong off both your reverse stick and your forehand stick. Shooting is understanding what shot is needed at that time based on where the defense is and how much time you have to execute the shot."

Familiarize yourself with shooting situations, and you'll more easily maintain your composure in a game. Incorporating the goal cage in drills during practice is an excellent time to experiment. When your coach calls for a shot on goal at the end of a drill, try something different every time. And don't underestimate the importance of practicing on your own in the backyard!

Visualization

Equally important to physical practice is mental practice. Take time each day to mentally review your role on the field. See the goal, see the corners you want to shoot for, and imagine yourself in various positions in the circle. Visualize yourself making different types of shots at different angles and aiming for different spots in the cage. Visualize the ball going into the cage.

Picture yourself entering the circle and releasing a clean, strong, quick hit. Imagine yourself following the shot with your stick on the ground as the shot bounces off the goalie's pads. You control the rebound with your stick and push the ball into the left corner of the cage. GOAL!!!

Next, think about receiving a pass on the stroke line, keeping the ball tight on your stick. Your body is positioned for a shot with your lead shoulder aimed at the goal. You flick the ball to the right of the goalie, tucking it into the back corner of the cage. Your stick is pointing to the perfect placement of your shot.

Create various scenes on the field and see yourself succeeding in each one. Write down these scenes to get a clear mental image of what will happen on the field. Says Coach Northcroft, "Write out a script of how you see yourself in the day and how you anticipate the day to be in competition or practice. See yourself doing things well and doing the things you're expected to do."

PUSHES AND FLICKS

Pushes and flicks are excellent shots because they involve no backswing—your stick is always on the ball from start to finish. A push is just as it sounds—you actually use the stick to push the ball forward without a backswing. With the push shot, you can send the ball in various directions without altering your body, which is deceptive to the goalie. Anywhere within the stroke line area of the cage is a good place to use the push shot. A flick is a similar motion, however, you lift the ball in the air instead of keeping it on the ground. A great time to use an aerial shot is if the goalie is down and you've rebounded the ball. Catching her off balance is always helpful. Stay low, keep your knees bent, and aim for the back corners of the cage.

Push

Developing a good push shot is important to any goal scorer. You are literally pushing the ball forward, using your body weight and momentum as strength for the push. Start with the ball on your stick in front of your back foot in the control box area. For forehand pushes, your right foot is your back foot. Put your weight on the ball of your rear foot, bend at the knees, and use the shake hands grip. Drop your right shoulder so your weight is behind the ball—this gives you more strength in your push and power in your shot. Align your left shoulder with the goal. Your right hand and arm are pushing the stick while your left hand is pulling the stick forward. Step with your front foot in the direction you want the ball to go as you push the ball forward. Keep your knees bent as you step and your eyes on the ball. As you transfer your weight to your front foot, point your toes to the goal and rotate your hips open so they face the goal. As your hips rotate, turn (or spin on) your back foot so your toes also point to the target. Keep your front knee bent when your weight transfers forward and your rear shoulder low. Your upper body will move forward as you transfer your

When you hit a push shot, the ball sits behind your front foot. This allows you to generate more power, since you don't take a backswing.

Rotate your hips as you release the shot to utilize the strength of your lower body.

weight to the front foot. It is important when this happens that you keep your rear shoulder low throughout the entire swing. Drive through the ball. If your shoulder pops up, you lose power and your shot will not be as fast or strong. Drop your shoulder and lower your right hand to produce more power from your upper body.

After the ball is released, point your stick at the target with the toe pointing up. To generate more speed on your push, bend deeper on your back leg and explode off of your rear foot.

Reverse Stick Push

When shooting the ball from your left side, use a reverse stick push. This is a difficult shot that takes a lot of practice to develop. Because the ball is on your left side, your right foot and shoulder are leading. The ball lies in front of your left foot on the toe of your stick. Hold the stick with both hands in the reverse grip. Drop your right shoulder and lower your right on the stick. The actual motion of the right hand and arm is more of a pull than a push.

Point your right shoulder at the target. Step off your back foot and onto your right (front) foot, pointing your right toes at the cage. Rotate your hips open to face the goal and pivot your rear foot so your toes point to the goal. Transfer all your weight to your front foot with your knees bent, staying low to the ground. Remember Northcroft's advice to keep your center of gravity low when shooting! Point your stick at the target with the toe pointing down on your follow-through swing.

DRAG PUSH

The drag push is best used on turf or other artificial surfaces. The smoother the surface, the better the speed of the push. As you dribble, keep the ball off your rear foot and shift your body into a shooting position. Drop your left shoulder and arm, lowering your stick so the handle is close to the ground in front of your left foot. The toe of the stick cradles the ball, with the flat side of the toe facing (and nearly touching) the ground. The hook of the stick wraps around the backside of the ball.

The strength of this shot comes from the shoulders and upper body, as well as your weight shift. Step forward with your left foot and drag the ball from behind you, hooked in the stick. As you drag, raise your left shoulder and the handle of your stick, keeping the ball hooked in the toe. Release the ball in front of your left foot and finish with your stick pointing at the goal cage. The speed generated from the drag causes the ball to fly toward the target. It is a fun, easy shot that is guaranteed to regularly find the back of the cage!

Flick

The flick is executed in a fashion similar to a forehand push, except the ball is lifted into the air. Position your body with your left foot and shoulder leading and your feet shoulder width apart. The ball is slightly ahead of your back foot.

Hold your stick in the shake hands grip with the face of the stick angled toward the sky. The bottom face of the toe is tucked under the lower half of the ball. Drop your right shoulder and bend your right elbow to get the stick underneath the ball. Step forward off your rear foot and point your left foot at the target. Swing your hips open and transfer your weight to the front foot as you did with the push, keeping your knees bent and your right shoulder level.

As your hips open and your weight shifts forward, lift the stick with the flat side facing the sky to elevate the ball. Use your right hand and wrist to provide energy to the flick and quickly turn it over to the left upon release. Once you lift the ball into the air, turn the stick over, so you are actually throwing the ball off the end of the stick. Keep the stick pointed toward your target to ensure the ball carries in that direction. Practice standing different distances from the ball. You may find that being a step farther away from the ball gives you greater leverage.

Set the stick behind the ball so the face leans back. This allows you to lift the ball in the air. Drop your rear shoulder and right hand on the stick, and finish high with your stroke. Aerial shots to the goaltender's stick side are difficult to stop.

QUICK HIT

The quick hit is a strong drive with a small backswing executed on the move from the dribbling position. The quick hit is a great shot to use from the top of the circle. It is a strong drive, but you are not pulling out of the dribble position to set up and there is no big backswing.

When dribbling with the ball on your strong right side, shift your body so your left foot and shoulder are lined up with the target. Keep your body low and never rise out of the dribbling position. As you shift, keep your knees bent, stay low to the ground, and keep your head over the ball. Slide your left hand down the handle from the shake hands grip so it is next to your right hand. Both hands are now halfway down the handle next to each other.

The strength of this hit is generated from the wrists. Remember Coach Shelton's tip to practice quick wrist snaps—this is where that will really come in handy. Hold the stick below your waist and cock your wrists back so the stick is straight out behind you, parallel to the ground. The toe is pointing straight up to the sky. Your arms are bent at the elbow and flexed, holding the stick poised. Step toward the goal with your leading left foot and transfer your weight to your front foot. Snap your wrists forward, shifting your arms but keeping your elbows bent, and drive the ball straight ahead. As you snap your wrists, the stick will come down so the face of the toe directly meets the ball in front of you. You want to hit the ball squarely, so the entire toe makes contact with the entire backside of the ball. Nothing feels better in hockey than getting off a solid hit. If you are hitting the ball with only part of the stick, you are probably not keeping your eyes on the ball.

As a result, the ball is not going as far or it is going in a different direction, straying from your target.

It is important that your upper body and head move with your body as your weight transfers to your front foot. Continue swinging so the stick is pointing toward the target in front of you and is parallel to the ground. Keep your head over the ball as you make contact. Don't lift your head up until after the ball has been hit.

Quick hits can also be executed when the ball is near your front foot. If you change the direction of your dribble, or don't have time to take another step, shoot the ball off your front foot. While shooting off your back foot gives you greater power, shooting off your front increases your accuracy. When shooting off your front foot, apply the same basic principles to the quick hit—strong sharp wrists, head over the ball, knees bent, and weight low. Because your weight is already on your front foot, however, there is no step forward.

As with all shots, aim for the corners of the cage. Know where the goalie is positioned and exploit the area of the goal that is uncovered.

CHIP SHOT

The chip shot is similar to a drive or a quick hit, except the ball is lifted into the air when it is hit. This is a great shot to use against a goalie, because it is an aerial shot with a ground hit setup. Unlike a flick, the goalie cannot determine that the ball is going to be in the air until after it is hit. This is a very difficult shot and should be practiced alone before attempting to use it in a game or practice situation.

The setup for the chip shot is similar to setting up for a quick hit—stay low, keep your head over the ball and your knees bent. When you pull your stick back to hit the ball, angle it so the toe is pointing behind you. Do this so that when you return the stick to the ball, the face will be slightly opened. This means that the toe is not square to the ball but is slightly facing the sky, as it is when you flick the ball. Aim to hit the lower half of the ball with the bottom of your stick, where the rounded edge meets the flat surface on the bottom of the toe. When you strike, the angle lifts the ball in the air, creating a strong, aerial drive. Don't forget to transfer your weight forward as you hit the ball to increase power and control.

EDGE SHOT

The edge shot is executed with either the outside or inside edge of your stick (the line where the rounded side meets the flat side). Pay attention to how you are holding your stick and make sure the right part of the stick is making contact with the ball. It is illegal to use the rounded side of the stick.

The best time to use the edge shot is from a dribble spin move. As discussed in this section, the spin move gives your body the momentum to make a strong edge shot. It also naturally positions your body behind the ball for a solid hit.

Although it is legal to use the outside edge of the stick, most edge shots are made with the inside edge. To execute an inside forehand edge shot, bend at the knees and lower your rear end so you are squatting. Place your feet wider than shoulder width apart. Your left foot is leading, and your left shoulder is pointing toward the goal. Your head and upper body are centered over your hips.

Hold your stick parallel to and touching the ground with the flat face down. Your hands start in a shake hands grip, but shift so the Vs of your right and left hands are pointing down the middle of the rounded side of the stick. Touch the ground with your knuckles. The ball rests in front of the lower area of your stick, the shaft. Start behind the ball and swing with your upper body, keeping the stick on the ground until the edge hits the ball. Shift your weight to your front foot. It is a good idea to practice this shot on your own and get comfortable with the motion of executing an edge shot from a straight dribble or spin dribble move.

Reverse Edge

The reverse edge shot is executed when the ball is on your left side. Bend deep at your knees and keep your feet wider than shoulder width apart. Center your head and upper body over your hips. Point your right foot (the lead foot) and your right shoulder to the target. Hold the stick parallel to and on the ground with the flat side facing the sky. The toe of your stick points toward the goal. With your knuckles contacting the ground, use the shake hands grip with the Vs of your hands centered down the flat side of the stick. Swing with your upper body and move the stick along the ground until the edge of the stick along the shaft contacts the ball, sending it toward the goal. Transfer your weight to your front foot, pointing your toes at the goal.

The reverse inside edge shot is great to use following a reverse spin move. With the ball on the toe of your stick, spin using the reverse stick to your right, dropping your right foot behind you to complete the circle. When you come around to the left side with the ball, drop down and position your body for a reverse edge shot. The spin move generates momentum for this shot.

DEFLECTION

A deflection is a shot that crosses in front of the cage and is redirected into the goal by the touch of a stick. Deflections often occur when the ball is hit into the circle across the front of the cage or when a slightly off-target shot is taken. In these cases, the offense must get a stick on the ball to redirect it into the cage. The most common deflection scenario is a right wing dribbling down the field to the right offensive corner and sending a strong drive across the circle, parallel to the end line, and about five to 10 yards in front of the goal. One teammate, usually someone on the front line, gets a stick on the ball and changes its path so it heads into the goal. A deflection is a one-touch redirection that happens so quickly the goalie has little or no time to react.

Timing is critical when making a deflected shot. Anticipate when the ball will be crossing in front of the cage and time your run into the circle accordingly. You do not want to be waiting in the middle of the circle for the ball—this gives the defense time to set up and intercept the ball. If your timing is off, backpedal or continue running through the circle and communicate with another team member to step in for the deflection. *Always* keep your feet moving in the circle and your toes pointing toward the cage.

You can deflect the ball into the cage by holding your stick either vertically or horizontally. Vertical deflections are used on grass fields because the vertical angle on your stick controls a ball that is bouncing off the ground. Use a forward push or jab with your stick to accelerate the speed of the deflection.

On an artificial surface, bend deep at your knees and hold your stick horizontally with your knuckles on the ground. Synthetic turf is smoother and the ball doesn't bounce as much, so the hits are faster and stronger. Holding your stick horizontally along the ground creates a larger surface area to deflect the ball when it is coming in at top speed.

From the Right

If the ball is coming from the right side, position your body so your left foot is leading and your left shoulder is pointing to the cage. The flat side of your stick faces where the ball is coming from, in this case the right side of the field. On grass, avoid using your reverse stick but rather position your body so (with your left foot leading) you are facing the ball as it approaches. Keep your feet wider than shoulder width apart, your knees bent, and your weight centered and balanced on the balls of your feet.

Hold your stick in a strong shake hands grip with your right hand lower for greater control. Keep your eyes on the ball. When the ball

One-time shots can catch the goalie out of position. Keep your body low so you can sweep the entire stick along the ground. It gives you a broader surface to redirect the pass.

reaches you, push or jab it in the direction of the cage to accelerate the deflection. As you do this, step with your left foot toward the cage, pointing your toes at the goal. Transfer your weight to your front foot as you step, maintaining your balance.

Always aim for the corner of the cage closest to where the ball is coming from, in this case the right corner of the cage. This way, the ball doesn't have as far to travel and the goalie has less time to react to the redirected shot.

On artificial turf, lead with your left foot and aim your left shoulder at the goal cage. There are two options when the ball is coming from the right side: use either a horizontal forehand or horizontal reverse grip. In both cases, face the source of the ball. When using a forehand grip, your left foot is ahead of the line the ball is traveling in. Hold the stick in the shake hands grip and lower your body so the entire stick is horizontally on the ground covering the space between your feet. Your knuckles are actually touching the turf, placing the entire stick on the ground, assuring that no ball will pass by you. As the ball approaches, step toward the cage, transferring your weight to your front foot and use the stick to sweep the ball into the cage.

With the reverse grip, your body is behind the line the ball is traveling on. Hold the stick in a reverse horizontal position on the ground with your knuckles on the turf. As you become more experienced and the speed of the game increases, hold the stick in the reverse grip with only your left hand (with knuckles on the turf) to deflect the ball. The toe of your stick points to where you want the ball to go. Keep your eyes on the ball until it connects with your stick.

From the Left

If the ball is coming from the left side of the field, lead with your right foot and aim your right shoulder at the goal. Stand with your feet shoulder width apart and bend deep at the knees. Keep your weight on the balls of your feet and your eyes on the ball.

On grass, hold the stick in a shake hands grip with the toe on the ground in front of your right foot. Your body is behind the line the ball travels on. As it approaches, step toward the cage with your front foot and deflect the ball when it is in front of your right foot. Follow through with a push or jab to accelerate the deflection.

On an artificial surface, lead with your right foot and point your right shoulder at the cage. Face the source of the ball and keep your body behind the line the ball will travel. Spread your feet wider than shoulder width and follow the ball with your eyes. Hold your stick in a shake hands grip and lower your upper body and arms so the stick is horizontally on the ground with your knuckles on the turf. The toe of your stick is in front of your right foot and angled so the toe is pointing to the corners of cage. Keep the entire stick on the ground and your knuckles touching the turf. As the ball arrives, push the stick forward to redirect the ball into the cage. As you become more experienced, use only your right hand on the stick, keeping your knuckles on the ground. This gives you a longer reach for the ball.

Another method of redirecting shots from the left side is to use the reverse grip. Widen your stance and lower your body to the ground. As the ball arrives, sweep your stick along the ground and hit the ball past the goalie.

DIVE SHOT

This shot is the most exciting to watch, and it takes the most guts to perform. Although there are strategies and tips for this shot, the best

With the goaltender coming out of her cage for the ball, you may not have time to reach the ball for a flick or push shot. In this situation, take to the air and try for a dive shot. It's your best chance of scoring and just might make the highlight tape.

advice for the dive shot is to keep your eye on the ball and follow your instincts.

A dive shot is performed when you are running for the ball and soon realize it's out of your reach. The momentum built by running at top speed gives you the fuel to execute this shot. Push off from the ground out of your run with your back foot and extend your body so it is parallel to the ground. Keep the toe of your stick on the ground and aim for the lower half of the ball. Hold the stick with either a forehand or reverse grip depending on where the ball is coming from. (Make sure the flat side of your stick is facing the ball.) When your stick reaches the ball, flick your wrists to redirect the ball into the cage. Wrist strength is instrumental in hitting this type of shot.

Keeping your eyes on the ball will naturally lead your stick to the right spot. Plan on a landing similar to a headfirst softball slide. Let the back of your forearms take the brunt of the fall followed by your midsection and upper thighs.

PENALTY SHOTS

Occasionally, the referee will blow the whistle because the defense has committed a severe penalty in the circle. When this happens, the offensive team is awarded a penalty shot. Examples of such a penalty include the goalie covering up the ball, catching the ball, or holding the ball with her glove, or a defensive player using her body to stop a shot from entering the cage.

All players leave the circle except for the goalie and one offensive player. The offensive team selects the shooter. The ball is placed on the penalty stroke line. The goalie stands with both feet behind the goal line in the cage. As the stroker, stand in position to the left of the ball, preparing to make a shot.

The best shot to use during a penalty stroke is a flick. It has a lot of power, and the ball can be directed high in the air or low to the ground. With the ball on the stroke line, position your body for the flick shot. The referee will ask you and the goalie if you are ready. Once you reply "yes," maintain that position until the whistle is blown. Your feet must remain stationary from the time you say you are ready until you actually make the shot. You may step with your left foot toward the cage when shooting, but your right foot must remain on the ground until after the shot.

Typically, the upper corners of the cage are the most difficult areas for the goalie to defend. The best spot is in the upper corner of her non-stick side. However, other high-percentage spots include either side of the goalie in line with her knees.

DIMENSIONS

The penalty stroke line is seven yards from the outside edge of the goal cage and 12 inches long. When shooting a stroke, you may place the ball anywhere along that 12-inch line. The goal cage is seven feet tall, 12 feet wide, and four feet deep. The hockey ball has a circumference ranging from 8 13/16 to 9 1/4 inches. Seems easy enough to get a ball that small into a cage that large, doesn't it?

DRILLS AND GAMES

Deflections

Players: Four
Equipment: Stick, balls, and goal cage, or cones set up as a goal cage
Distance: Shooting circle, or 16 yards

Form two lines at the top of the circle opposite the left and right posts of the cage. Two players will be outside the circle on the far right and far left, each with a pile of balls about 10 yards from the end line. On command, the hitter on the right will drive the ball across the circle in front of the goal cage. At the same time, the first player in each of the two lines sprints into the circle, breaking down their steps as they approach the path of the ball. The players must communicate with each other to say who is going for the ball. Naturally, the player on the side closest to the ball will be first in line to get it. As the ball crosses in front of the first player, she deflects it into the cage using either a vertical or horizontal stick, depending on the ground surface. Once the first ball is hit and deflected in, the shooters backpedal to the top of the circle. When they reach the top of the circle the left-side hitter drives the ball across the circle as the shooters spring forward, again racing to deflect the ball into the cage. After the ball is deflected, the shooters again backpedal to the top of the circle to repeat the deflection from the right side. Alternate sides and take two hits from each side. When finished, switch roles so the hitters are now deflecting and the shooters become the hitters.

Follow That Shot!

Players: One and goalie
Equipment: Stick, ball, cage, goalie equipment, mouth guards
Distance: Shooting circle, 16 yards

Start at the 25-yard line and dribble to the circle. When you reach the top of the circle, shoot the ball on cage with a quick hit. Practice shooting from the dribble—don't allow yourself extra time to set up because you won't have that time in a game situation. Once the ball is released, follow your shot with two hands on the stick and break down your footwork as you approach the goalie. Anticipate where she is going to clear the ball. Collect the rebound and shoot again using a push, flick, or edge shot.

This is good work for the shooter and the goalie and can be repeated as many times as needed. To make it more demanding and create a more gamelike situation, time yourself from when you shoot the ball. Allow no more than 20 seconds to shoot the ball, collect the rebound, and shoot again.

Coach's Tip: Make this a game by keeping track of goalie clears and shots scored.

Rapid Fire Deflection and Follow

Players: At least four, useful for entire team practice
Equipment: Ball, goal cage, sticks, goalie equipment, shin guards, and mouth guards
Distance: Shooting circle, 16 yards

One player is in the center of the circle near the stroke line. The goalie is in the cage, prepared to block shots. All other players stand around the circle, each with a ball. The first player on the far right side of the circle shoots the ball on goal. The player in the center deflects it into the cage. If the goalie blocks the shot, the player in the center goes for the rebound and continues shooting until the goalie clears the ball from the circle. Once the ball is cleared or a shot has been scored, the next player in line on the circle shoots on goal and the player in the center again deflects it into the cage. Continue until all players on the circle have shot their balls. Spread out around the circle so the player in the middle is getting shots from all angles. Rotate once all shots have been taken so a new player is in the center of the circle. Wear your shin guards and mouth guards!

Shots on Goal

Players: One
Equipment: Stick, five balls, goal cage, two cones, masking tape
Distance: Vary 16 yards, 10 yards, seven yards

From the left post of the goal, move 12 inches in along the goal line toward the center of the cage and place one cone on the ground. Do the same from the right side, placing one cone 12 inches in toward the center of the cage along the goal line.

Create two triangles in the upper left and right corners of the cage. Start at the top right corner and move 12 inches down the post. Mark the spot. Again at the top right corner, move in 12 inches along the top crossbar and mark the spot. These two marks create two legs of your triangle. From those two marks, use the masking tape to create the third leg of the triangle, which should also be about 12 inches long. Do the same thing in the top left corner of the cage.

Line up five balls along the 16-yard line, leaving about 12 inches between balls. Start at the ball farthest to the left and one at a time drive the balls into the cage. Aim for the corners and keep track of how many go into the cage. For each ball that goes into the goal between the two cones in the middle 10 feet, give yourself one point. If your shot enters the smaller area marked off by the cones in the left and right corners of the cage, give yourself three points.

Move up so you're 10 yards from the cage and line the balls up in a similar fashion. Push the balls into the goal. Aim for the corners. Score yourself using the same point system as above.

Now place all five balls along the penalty stroke line. Flick the balls, aiming for the sides of the cage and the top corner triangles. Keep track of your points, allotting five points for every ball that goes into the cage through the triangle. Keep track of your points and aim to improve your score every time you do this drill.

Endurance in Shooting

Players: One and goalie
Equipment: Stick, five balls, five cones, goalie equipment, and goal cage
Distance: Shooting circle, 16 yards

Place one cone at the top of the circle with the pile of five balls. Set a second cone five yards to the right of the center cone and a third cone five yards to the left of the center cone. The fourth cone is five yards to the left of the left goal post on the end line, and the fifth cone is five yards to the right of the right goal post on the end line.

The goalie stands in the center of the cage, and the shooter stands at the top of the circle at the center cone with one ball. Starting at the same time, the shooter dribbles around the cone to the right and back to the center cone, while the goalie shuffles over to the cone to her left, touching the cone and returning to the goal cage. When the dribbler returns to the center cone, she shoots the ball from the top of the circle. The goalie must hustle to get back to the cage to block the shot.

Once the shooter has shot the ball, she grabs another ball with her stick and dribbles around the cone to the left. The goalie, once she has blocked the first shot, shuffles to the cone to her right, touches it, and returns to the cage to block the next shot.

Repeat this until all five balls are gone, alternating between the left- and right-side dribbles and shuffles. When starting, the dribbler should not use a reverse stick but rather get her feet around, keeping a strong forehand grip. After practicing this method, move on to using the reverse stick when dribbling and shooting. Focus on the mechanics of your shot—keep your head over the ball, transfer your weight forward, stay low to the ground, and snap your wrists cleanly to get off a strong hit.

Practicing Variety

Players: One and goalie (if available)
Equipment: One stick, five balls, two cones, goal cage, goalie equipment
Distance: Shooting circle, 16 yards

Line the five balls up 10 yards in front of the goal cage. Place one cone slightly outside and opposite the left post in line with the penalty stroke, and one cone slightly outside and opposite the right post in line with the penalty stroke. Start at the center with the balls and dribble one ball around the cone to the left, spinning or dribbling around it.

When you come to the outside, shoot the ball with a reverse push, edge shot, or some variation of a reverse stick shot. Be creative. Sprint back to the pile of balls in the middle and dribble again to the cone to the right. Dodge the cone, and when you come to the outside, shoot the ball with a quick hit, flick, or push. Do a different shot every time and practice shooting off your front foot too. Always keep your stick on the ball and shoot as soon as you get around the cone. Time yourself to get all five shots off. Aim to decrease your time every time you do this drill.

6
TACKLING

Imagine the left wing on the opposing team picks up a long hit from her defense and is heading down the field on a fast breakaway. Our defensive heroine (that's you) chases her down. The crowd is going wild. You break down your steps, close in on the dribbler, and execute a clean defensive tackle, gaining control of the ball and sending a sharp pass to an open teammate up field. You have saved the day. Feel free to picture yourself with a red cape and a gold headband if it helps complete the image.

WHAT IS TACKLING?

Tackling is one of the most important defensive elements in field hockey. It is necessary to emphasize, however, that it is a skill used by every player on the field from the deep defensive sweeper to the high scoring center forward. An effective tackle means that you disrupt the flow of the dribbling opponent, remove the ball from her possession, and overtake possession of the ball.

There are three basic types of tackling in field hockey: the

When a great dribbler squares off against a great tackler, it creates one of the most exciting battles in field hockey.

jab tackle, the block tackle, and the recovery tackle. The jab tackle is used to knock, or jab, the ball away from a dribbling opponent and gain control of the ball. The block tackle is used to literally block the forward progress of the ball from a dribbling opponent. The recovery tackle, as the name indicates, is used when a dribbler has moved into the space behind you (as described in the opening scene of the chapter) and you must run back and recover defensively.

Regardless of the tackle, Coach Morett has some advice. "I tell our players they need to be determined, persistent, disciplined, aggressive, and poised. There are so many ingredients that go into playing great individual defense. Individual defense is having an attitude to stay disciplined and keep your opponent and the ball in front of you."

Judging Distance to the Ball

Certain principles hold true regardless of which tackle you use on defense. One of those principles is judging distance. To properly execute any tackle, you must accurately judge the distance between yourself, your opponent, and the ball. Consider your stick an extension of your body, and understand how that influences your reaching distance. Know how close or far you have to be to make contact with the ball without missing it because you couldn't reach it (too far) or accidentally hitting your opponent or her stick (too close). This is called hacking and is a penalty. When executing a tackle, aim to be about one stick length away from the dribbler.

HACKING

The most common defensive penalty committed when tackling is hacking. Hacking occurs when the defense throws the stick into the dribbler's path, attempting to jab tackle the ball. However, the defensive stick, instead of hitting the ball, comes in contact with the offense's stick. This is a penalty that is almost always caught by the officials because of the noise the two sticks make when they come in contact. The penalty for hacking is a free hit for the offensive team.

Your best bet to avoid hacking is to remain patient and wait for the ball to come off the dribbler's stick, moving with her as she dribbles down the field. Strengthening your left wrist will also give you greater control of your stick movement and prevent unnecessary flailing of the stick, which could result in hacking.

Forcing to the Outside —Use a Lead Foot

Having successfully judged distance, position your body so you force the dribbler toward the outside of the field. Accomplish this by staying on the goal side of the dribbler. To understand exactly what this means, draw an imaginary line between the goal you are defending and the opponent with the ball. Standing goal side means you position yourself on this line with your back to the cage. Face the dribbler slightly to the left or right of her, depending on which side of the field you're on. The important thing is that you face her and she is closer to the sideline. You never want to be behind your opponent.

When a player is dribbling down the right side of the field, lead with your left foot to push her toward the sideline and away from the goal cage.

Establishing a lead foot helps position your body appropriately. If, for example, the dribbler is coming down your left side, use your right foot as a lead. Lead in with your right shoulder and square up to your opponent's left shoulder. If you were to continue walking along the imaginary line drawn from the cage, you would walk right into your opponent and literally be forcing her off the field.

Regardless of the side you're on, never let the ball past your lead foot. This positioning allows your body to react quickly if your opponent makes cuts or changes direction. When executing a tackle, step quickly and lightly on your lead foot, keeping your weight on the balls of your feet.

A common tackling mistake is to step with all your weight toward the ball and miss it, losing your balance and agility. This is called "overcommitting" and allows your opponent to pass you and get in the space behind you. Coach Morett agrees. "We have a lot of missed tackles when a player's body is off balance. Not only do they miss a tackle but they can't recover because their body is off balance. Footwork and a balanced body position are probably the most important steps to executing any type of skill with the stick."

Stay patient and tackle when the ball comes off the dribbler's stick. Always aim for the lower half of the ball with your stick when tackling.

Doing this ensures that you are steering away from the opponent's stick and not hacking. Being underneath the ball also provides you with enough leverage to effectively lift and redirect the ball to recover possession. Keep your weight on the balls of your feet and stay balanced. To sum it up in the words of Coach Shelton: "Keep your feet moving and don't commit."

The above principles will be repeated in each description of the different tackles because they are essential to each technique. Master these rudimentary skills and you're on your way to becoming a proficient tackler.

THE JAB TACKLE

The jab tackle is a great tackle to use anywhere on the field. Most jabs are executed with just the left hand because it increases your reaching distance to the ball. The purpose of the jab is to knock the ball away from your dribbling opponent and gain possession.

Position your body so your knees are bent, your feet are slightly more than shoulder width apart, and your weight is predominantly on the balls, or power points, of your feet. In this position, you can react quickly to an opponent's sudden move in any direction. On the hockey field, if you're standing still too long, your heels grow roots. It's going to be that much harder to get moving, so stay active.

Position your body in the defensive stance with two hands on the stick. Bend your knees until the toe of your stick touches the ground. Do not simply bend at the back. Make sure to stick your rear end out as if you're about to sit down. This may feel uncomfortable at first, but you'll get used to it. Do you feel your thighs burning a little? If so, you're in the correct position. As a defender, it is important to stay low to the ground. Being low to the ground keeps you focused on the ball and lowers your center of gravity, which increases your balance and reaction time.

Assuming you're defending on the right side of the field, square your shoulders to your opponent's right shoulder. Lead with your left foot to keep her close to the right sideline and don't let the ball pass your lead foot.

When the ball comes off the dribbler's stick, quickly extend your stick with your left hand and jab the ball. The advantage of using the one-handed jab is that you have a much longer reach than you otherwise would with your right hand on the stick. Aim to hit the lower half of the ball with the bottom edge of your stick (where the toe face meets the rounded edge). Keep the rounded side of the toe of your stick on the ground and the face of the stick pointing up to the sky. You want to get under the ball and quickly jab it away from the opponent in a small scooping motion.

Step quickly and lightly on your lead foot when jabbing. Once your arm and stick are completely extended and you've tapped the lower part of the ball, recoil back to the shake hands grip with the toe of your stick on the ground in front of your feet. If you've successfully knocked the ball away from your opponent, use this grip to control the ball, dribble, and pass to an open teammate. It is much stronger than the left-handed grip. From the left side of the field, use the reverse V grip. Lead with your right foot but make sure that you're one step ahead of the dribbler to avoid a penalty. The reverse side tackle is more

The jab tackle is as much about timing as it is about technique. As the ball comes off the dribbler's stick, jab at the ball with your stick to poke the ball from your opponent's control.

difficult to execute because you are reaching across your opponent and will need more room to cleanly contact the ball without hitting her.

At times, your opponent will maintain possession after you jab the ball. This is not a failure. This is defense. Move with your opponent and continue jabbing, keeping your eyes on the ball. This is incredibly frustrating to the dribbler and will often get you the ball. At the very least, you'll be slowing her down and giving your teammates time to recover and help you out defensively.

In the circle, use a two-hand jab. The game is different in the circle than on the rest of the field. It's a lot more crowded, so you really have to control your body. There are two reasons to use the two-handed jab. First, the two-hand grip gives you greater stick control so you're more likely to hit the ball and not your opponent's stick. Secondly, after you've jabbed the ball you can quickly recoil back and place your stick on the ground. Coach Morett says, "If the other team is coming into our attacking circle, then our players need to make sure their sticks are flat on the ground and they're blocking space with their sticks." It is important to play clean defense in the circle because any defensive fouls will result in a corner penalty—an offensive advantage.

Practice Makes Perfect

The only way to improve this tackle, and any tackle, is to practice. First begin practicing on your own and get comfortable with the ball and the feel of the jab movement. When you develop confidence in your jabbing skills, practice with a partner who is dribbling the ball. The trick here is to keep your eyes on the ball and only the ball. What your opponent's feet are doing or where her stick is moving is irrelevant and will only confuse you. Concentrate on the ball and use your stick to knock it out of her possession.

STRENGTHENING EXERCISES

Wall Sits
A solid defensive position in field hockey requires some training. To improve your body positioning, do wall sits. Stand with your back against the wall and your feet about one foot away from the wall. Slide down the wall until you are in a sitting position and your thighs form a right angle with the wall. Your knees should also form a right angle between your calves and thighs. Be sure to move your feet out so your knees aren't extending over your toes. Hold this position for 30 seconds. Stand up and rest for 30 seconds to one minute and start again. Increase the hold time in this position as you gain strength in your thighs.

Wrist Strengthening

Equally important to increasing your leg strength is increasing your wrist strength. The left hand is the dominant hand in field hockey. If you're like 90 percent of the population, you are right-handed, so strengthening your left hand is an issue that must be addressed. Hold the stick straight out in front of you with only your left hand on the grip and the toe pointing directly forward. Hold for 30 seconds. Slowly move the stick so the toe is pointing to the left of you with your arm still fully extended. The stick is parallel to the ground and perpendicular to your arm. Hold for 30 seconds. Point the toe to the right and hold again. Do this a few times a day; increase your holding time as your strength improves.

THE BLOCK TACKLE

The block tackle, like the jab tackle, can be used anywhere on the field and requires balance, patience, and control. The block tackle is a good defense to use against someone who is speed dribbling or power dribbling. It's very important to accurately judge the distance between yourself, your opponent, and the ball to execute a successful block tackle.

The block tackle movement must be quick and precise. The actual blocking action involves the stick to either be vertically or horizontally angled toward the ground so the ball is trapped when it comes off the opponent's stick.

When you are making contact with the ball, let your stick give lightly with the ball. As discussed in chapter 4, Passing and Receiving, if you don't let your stick give, the ball will bounce back toward the opponent, giving her an opportunity to regain control. Be careful not to swing at the ball, as this will also send the ball off your stick. Timing is a key element of block tackling. As you are waiting for the right time to block tackle, throw a few jabs at the dribbler to fluster her. When you are ready to make the tackle, shift your body from a defensive position into one of the following moves: a vertical block tackle position, a horizontal forehand block tackle position, or a horizontal reverse block tackle position.

Vertical Block Tackle

The vertical block tackle is used most frequently on grass fields. This is because the ball is more likely to bounce off the ground due to

Always keep your stick in front of your legs when using the vertical block tackle. It keeps the ball from hitting your feet.

bumps in the playing surface. To assume the vertical block tackle position, bend your knees and hold your weight on the balls of your feet, similar to the jab tackle position. Your stance, however, is narrower—your feet are positioned shoulder width apart with your left foot leading if the dribbler is on your right side.

Hold your stick in the shake hands grip to the left of your stomach; your right hand grips the stick near your left knee and the toe of your stick rests on the ground in front of your right foot, parallel to your left foot. Hold your left hand farther away from your body so that your stick is angled to the ground. Keeping the stick in front of your legs and your feet will prevent the ball from bouncing off the ground into your body. Stay low and balanced on the balls of your feet so you can react to the dribbler. The vertical tackle is commonly used when the dribbler has no choice but to dribble forward.

Angle your stick toward the ground. When receiving or intercepting a ball, this angle causes the ball to drop down in front of you. This is an important point to keep in mind at all times during the game. If your stick is angled away from the ground, it acts as a ramp and the ball can easily be launched into either yourself or another player.

Forehand Horizontal Block Tackle

The forehand horizontal tackle is used more often on artificial surfaces because they are smoother and the ball doesn't lift off the ground

On smooth playing surfaces, the horizontal block tackle is very effective. It's important that you bend at the waist, not just the knees.

(unintentionally, at least) as much. There are two types of horizontal block tackles: forehand and reverse. Determine which type to use by the position of the dribbler. If she is facing you on your right side, use the forehand block tackle.

The forehand block tackle requires you to be low to the ground. With both hands on the stick, bend your knees and your waist and lower your arms until your stick is horizontal to the ground and your knuckles are touching the ground. Angle your stick toward the ground so you won't have that nasty ramp that could send the ball flying. Point your stick slightly away from you, at a two o'clock angle. Spread your feet nearly the length of the stick apart, with your left foot leading. Remember to bend at the waist, not just at your knees. As always, keep your weight on the balls of your feet so you can quickly move in any direction.

As the dribbler approaches, keep your eyes on the ball. When it comes off her stick, firmly hold your stick along the ground in the horizontal block tackle position described above. The stick is completely on the ground in the space in front of the dribbler. The stick traps the ball because the flat surface of the stick is angled slightly to the ground. Control the ball on your stick and pass to an open teammate. The dribbler will likely run right past you.

Reversing It

For the reverse block tackle, position your body in the same way as the forehand tackle, but this time your right foot is leading and your left foot is lined up with the ball. Use the reverse V grip on the stick and lower your body so the stick is horizontal to the ground. Extend the

If a player attempts to dribble past your left side, use the reverse horizontal block tackle. Touch the ground with your knuckles and angle your stick toward the ground to trap the ball.

stick straight out so its top (the handle) is in front of your left foot. Touch the dirt with your knuckles and bend your right knee so it is almost touching the ground. Make sure to angle the stick toward the ground to trap the ball.

As you become a more experienced player, begin using the reverse tackle with just your left hand. This takes strength, experience, and confidence. By just using your left hand, you can increase your reach and react quicker to a change in the dribbler's direction.

Using the Sidelines

The horizontal tackle is very effective when used with a sideline. It gives the dribbler no room to dodge you. If she's coming down your left side, stay in her line to the cage. Use the reverse tackle along the sideline to secure the ball. The same applies if she is dribbling down the right side of the field. Keep your body in her line to the goal and use the forehand tackle along the sideline.

WORKING TOGETHER—THE L TRAP

An excellent time to use the block tackle is if one of your teammates is defending the dribbler and forcing her in your direction. Talk to your teammate and let her know you're there to help. She can lead the dribbler right into your stick. When the time is right, use the block tackle to take the ball away from the dribbler. Coach Shelton refers to this double-teaming as the L trap. She says the L trap is "basically a double team where you channel into a person and that person comes with their stick to form an L (or sometimes V) to come up with the ball."

THE RECOVERY TACKLE

Despite all of your fabulous defensive efforts, every now and then the ball will get past you. When this happens, it is time for you to recover quickly and stop the opponent from getting closer to your goal. To do this, sprint back to the dribbler. When sprinting to recover in field hockey, hold your stick in your right hand only and pump your arms to gain maximum speed. The most important part of the recovery tackle is getting back in a defensive position.

Because your opponent is dribbling, you should be able to catch her quickly. To illustrate this point, stand at the 50-yard line with a teammate. As she speed dribbles the ball to the end line, sprint with your stick in your right hand. Start at the same time and see how much faster you are without the ball. This is your defensive advantage in the recovery tackle.

When recovering, keep the opponent on the outside of the field. Make sure that you are sprinting back on the side of her that is closest to the goal cage. Once you overtake her, use your body positioning and

When chasing down a player who has gotten behind you, run to the goal side. In this case, the player is dribbling down the right side of the field, so the defender recovers to tackle her from the left side.

stick to continue forcing her to the outside of the field and away from the cage.

Patience

Patience is integral when recovering. Do not tackle your opponent from behind. You'll only receive a penalty and put your team at a disadvantage. And as tempting as it may be, don't run directly at the dribbler and lunge at the ball and overcommit. One minor body fake from her and she'll blow right past you.

To properly recover and defend your opponent, run until you're one step ahead of her and in line with the ball. Once you start closing in on her, break down your steps to get yourself under control. Bring your stick and body back to a defensive position with two hands on the stick and the toe of your stick on the ground. Lower your body closer to the ground, abandoning the straightened posture you had when you were sprinting.

Continue forcing the dribbler to the outside of the field. As you run alongside her, throw some jabs at the ball. Use a block tackle to gain control if the ball comes off her stick. The recovery tackle is actually any combination of the jab and/or block tackle. What distinguishes the recovery tackle is the fact that you are moving at top speed. You are still using the left-handed jab, keeping your eyes on the ball and aiming for the lower half of the ball. Once you knock it out of her possession, control the ball and shift to an offensive mindset.

Recovering on the right side is much easier than recovering on the left side of the field. Your body naturally assumes a defensive position when you're recovering on the right side. The left side requires a bit more speed and dexterity because the tackle is executed with the reverse stick. Recover alongside the opponent, containing her along the sideline. Hold your stick in the reverse grip and lower your body to a tackling position. When the time is right and the ball is off her stick, use your reverse stick to jab or block tackle to intercept her dribble. You're still moving, so don't step into her and overcommit yourself. Be assertive but remain patient.

DRILLS AND GAMES

Keep Your Eye on the Ball

Players: One
Equipment: Stick and ball
Distance: 50 yards

Line up on the end line with a stick and a ball. Position your body as described for the jab tackle. Step forward with your left foot and jab the ball with your stick in your left hand. Aim for the lower half of the ball and move it forward. Quickly recoil, returning the right hand to the stick and standing in the defensive position. Move to where the ball is and prepare to jab again. Continue doing this left-handed jab and recoil until you reach the 50-yard line. Take your time and do this right; it is not a race.

This drill improves your hand/stick coordination when jab tackling. It also helps you understand what area of the ball you're aiming for and how to effectively move it quickly with just the left hand. By continuing to perform exercises that involve the left hand only, you will strengthen the left hand and wrist, which ultimately provides you with greater stick and ball control.

By returning to the defensive position with both hands on the stick immediately after jabbing the ball, you train your body to stay low with two hands on the stick and the toe on the ground.

The Opposite Game

Players: Two
Equipment: Stick and ball
Distance: Five-yard-by-five-yard grid

This exercise is good for players who are already comfortable with the jab tackle. In the five-yard grid, two players face each other, preparing to go one on one. The offense starts with the ball on one sideline. Her goal is to pass over the opposite sideline. The defender holds her stick backwards so that the toe is in her left hand and the handle is on the ground. The defense's job is to stop the offense from making it through the grid by jabbing the ball away with the stick handle.

This game trains the defender to keep her eye on the ball. Timing and aim have to be precise; there is no longer a large toe surface with which to hit the ball.

Practicing the Block

Players: At least two
Equipment: Stick and ball
Distance: 25 yards

Two teammates stand facing each other about 25 yards apart. One player speed dribbles in a straight line, the other runs toward the dribbler and breaks down her steps as she approaches. The defender works on positioning her body and judging the distance to the ball and the dribbler. Once she is in a defensive position, she executes a forehand block tackle and controls the ball. The two players should intermittently switch roles. When the players feel comfortable in this skill, work on the reverse block tackle by having the dribbler approach on the left side of the defender.

As players improve and become more comfortable with the block tackle, have the dribbler incorporate some dodges in her approach. Confine the dribbling space to a five- to 10-yard wide area, still using the 25-yard length distance.

Coach's Tip: Split the team in two lines and have the players go one at a time against each other. The advantage of having just one offensive and one defensive player go at a time is that the coach can point out to the group when a tackle is performed correctly. Once you've seen all your players go through and feel comfortable with their understanding of the tackle, split the lines into two groups on different sides of the field, or pair the players up one on one, so the drill moves faster.

Tag—You're It!

Players: At least two
Equipment: Just your body
Distance: 15 yards

Leave the sticks and balls behind and stand facing each other about 15 yards apart. One player will act as the offense, one as the defense. The two players run toward each other at the same time. The defender breaks down her steps as the two approach each other and gets in front of the offensive player so that she cannot sprint past her. Practice judging the distance to your opponent and positioning your body accordingly. This resembles a basketball-style positioning when opponents face each other one on one. The defender should keep her body positioning low so she has good balance. The offense should try to use fakes to throw the defender. She can use spin moves or fake with her head, upper body, feet, or a combination of all of the above.

The goal for the defender in this game is to tag the backside of the offense's knees by reaching around her opponent. The trick for the defense is to stay in front of the opponent despite her spins and body fakes. Defensive players learn to stay low and focus on the midsection of the opponent. If a defender is looking at the upper body or feet of her opponent, she'll get beat. By keeping the offense in front of her, the defender is maintaining her defensive positioning and learning how to control her body. The tag does not count if the offense successfully runs away from the defender.

Offense and defense must both learn that the body is just as important in playing field hockey as are the stick and ball. Offense will become adept at using body fakes to outsmart the opponent.

The game is over once the defender tags the offense's knees or once the offense gets past the defender untouched. The two players then switch roles.

Coach's Tip: Keep score of how many times the offense runs by untouched and how many times the defense tags the offense's knees. This paints a clear picture of areas the team needs to work on.

Recovery Drills

Players: At least two
Equipment: Stick and ball
Distance: 50 or 25 yards

One player is standing on the 50-yard line with her back to the goal. The other is facing the goal with the ball on the 40- or 45-yard line (the appropriate distance will be determined once the drill is completed once or twice), slightly to the side of the player on the 50.

When commanded, the offense begins speed dribbling toward the goal. At the same time, the defense turns around and sprints back toward the dribbler, forcing her away from the goal and performing a recovery tackle. If the defense is catching the offense without much effort, move the lines farther apart.

Switch the defensive line to the opposite side of the offensive line so recovery tackles can be performed on both the left and right sides of the field.

Coach's Tip: Ideally, the defense will recover beautifully and gain control of the ball. If the dribbler makes it into the circle, however, she should shoot on goal, giving the goalie a workout and allowing the defender and goalie to practice working together.

GOAL KEEPING

"I always tell my goalkeepers that we want to make a play on the ball rather than being played by the ball or the situation. If you have the opportunity to step up and make a play rather than being a sitting duck on the end line, do it."

—Penn State University goalie coach Jon O'Haire

Good goalies have quick reflexes and a fearless attitude. They tend to be outgoing, loud, fun, and quick-witted. Often, they are everyone's favorite player on the team. A goalie thrives under pressure and loves a good challenge. She is athletic, brave, and agile, and has lightning-fast reflexes.

A goalkeeper's cage is her home. She takes pride in her territory near the end of the field and protects it with every ounce of energy.

RESPONSIBILITIES

The goalie's number-one responsibility is to stop the ball from crossing over the goal line and into the cage. In the defensive circle, the goalie uses her stick, hands, feet, or any other body part to block the ball from entering the goal. But these powers cease to exist as soon as the goalie steps out of the defensive circle. Once outside the circle, the same rules apply to the goalie as they do to the rest of the players on the field.

Because goalies are constantly in danger of being hit by the ball—with some shots traveling in excess of 100 miles per hour at advanced

The goaltender must see and direct all from behind her mask in the cage. She is truly the last line of defense.

levels of play—goalies wear special protective gear. Never play the goalie position—even in practice—without the entire protective outfit (helmet with face mask, mouth guard, neck guard, chest guard, gloves, leg pads, and kickers) worn in place.

As the goalie, you have a view of the entire field, and therefore the best understanding of what is happening in the game. You are responsible for organizing and directing the defense in the backfield. When you see players from the other team who are unmarked, call out their numbers and alert your defense to mark up.

Always maintain a clear view of the ball. If a defender is blocking your view, tell her to get out of the way. You can't block what you can't see.

Body Positioning

Once you strap on all your gear, you must think, act, and move like a goalie. The proper goalie stance is a ready position with your toes facing forward and your knees bent. Bending your knees lowers your center of gravity and provides improved balance. Lean forward slightly with your upper body so your weight is on the balls of your feet. Align your chin with your bent knees, and align your bent knees with your toes. Check to make sure your body is in the proper alignment.

Bend your elbows and hold your arms out to your sides, palms facing forward. Hold your stick halfway down the shaft in your right hand so the flat side of the stick faces forward. The stick is an extension of the goalie's right arm. Use the stick to save a shot, but never swing at the ball with your stick. You'll be whistled for a violation.

When you move around the circle, stay on the balls of your feet and stay poised. Take quick, short steps to maintain your balance. Always keep your shoulders and body square to the ball.

Angles

Proper positioning is key to blocking shots. When the other team is approaching the circle, don't sit back and wait for the ball to come to you. Play aggressively. The goal line is your starting point, but you must come off the goal line about two or three yards at an angle to the shooter in order to block the shot. By coming out of the cage toward the ball, you'll cut down the shooter's angle, making it more difficult for the shooter to get the ball in the goal. "You don't want a goalkeeper who stays on the goal line to defend the goal. With the equipment, skill, and privileges goalkeepers have inside the circle, they can break up a play where others can't," says Coach O'Haire.

The shooter has the widest angle at the top of the circle. The greater the angle the shooter has on cage, the farther you come out to block the shot. The closer the shooter is to the end line, the less of an angle she'll have for a shot. If the shooter is positioned near the endline, stay close to the goal line and near the goalpost on the same side from which she's shooting.

To determine how far to come out of the cage, draw an imaginary line from the center of the back of the cage to the position of the ball. When the ball enters the circle, step out of the cage toward the ball along this line. By coming out of the cage at this angle, you are diminishing the shooter's angle on goal and reducing her vision of the cage.

Now envision a semicircle on the ground in front of the cage with its endpoints at each goalpost. If the circle were complete, the goal line between the posts would be the diameter of the circle. The semicircle in front of the cage indicates how far you come out of the cage on your angle to the ball. Combine this semicircle line with the line you have drawn from the back of the cage to the ball. Step out along the imaginary line from the back of the cage to the ball, and stop where that line intercepts with the imaginary semicircle formed between the two posts.

When the ball is near the end line to your right, stand next to your right post and face the ball. As you move into this position next to the post, use your stick to feel for where the post is so you don't have to take your eyes off the ball. Stand right up against the post so your leg pad is slightly in front of and up against the post. This keeps the ball from getting between you and the goalpost.

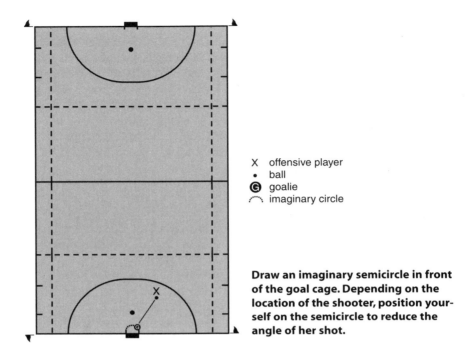

X offensive player
• ball
Ⓖ goalie
⌒ imaginary circle

Draw an imaginary semicircle in front of the goal cage. Depending on the location of the shooter, position yourself on the semicircle to reduce the angle of her shot.

When moving to the left post (when the shooter is along the end line to the left of you), use your left hand to feel for the post. Position your body with your left leg pads up against and in front of the post.

When faced with a situation where there is just one or no other defenders back, come out of the cage beyond the semicircle line to pressure the shooter and get the ball. "Goalkeepers must recognize opportunities where they can use their abilities to break up plays before they become shots on goal. They must learn to be more comfortable playing off of the goal line," says Coach O'Haire. "But," he continues, "there is a time and place for coming out for the ball. There are situations where a keeper will be more effective staying in the goal, especially when she has defenders back. In goalkeeping, not everything works every single time. You have to read the situation and know when you can come off line or when you can stay back."

Footwork

To improve your mobility around the circle, focus on footwork. "Goalkeepers need to move and execute a skill at the same time. Most balls are played with the feet. If you run to a point but can't kick the ball, you've got a problem. Footwork allows you to step up to a place and execute a skill when you get there," says Coach O'Haire.

When you move around the circle, take small steps to alter your angles. If you take large steps, the shooter can hit the ball through your legs. Keep your weight forward on your toes and step quickly and lightly on the balls of your feet. Never turn your back to the play, but use shuffle or drop steps to reposition as you change your angles.

Keep your knees bent, shoulders square, and toes facing the ball. Don't allow your stronger foot to dominate your play. "You need to be able to kick with both the left and right foot," advises Coach O'Haire. "Spend additional time working to increase the strength of your weaker foot."

GAINING FLEXIBILITY

The more flexible you are as a goalie, the better your ability to react and make the incredible save. You can increase your overall flexibility by stretching every day before and after every practice. Do not stretch when your muscles are cold. Go for a light jog first to get your muscles loose before you stretch to avoid injury. Take your time with your stretching and make sure that you work every muscle group.

Coach O'Haire suggests that goalies practice yoga. "Yoga is a good thing because it allows goalkeepers to focus on the body. Flexibility is a physical skill—just like you work on strength, you must work on flexibility. You've got to be able to stretch to cover the corners of the cage," he says.

BLOCKS

Goalies use different blocking techniques to stop the ball. These methods vary depending on size, skill, and ability. The basic philosophy for beginners is to "get your body behind the ball, control it down, and clear it," says Coach O'Haire.

The best way to develop your blocking skill is to constantly work hard and try different blocks in practice. Focus on individual footwork drills to warm up, and then participate in any drills that conclude with shots on cage during your team practice.

Standard Block

The most common block to a straight shot on the ground is to get your body centered in front of the shot and use your leg pads to block it.

For the standard block, keep your feet together and lean your weight forward. Hold your glove and stick out to the side and keep your eyes on the ball at all times.

When blocking a shot, always keep your feet together and your leg pads up against each other, eliminating space between your feet and your legs.

Start in the ready position and move toward the shooter to cut off her angle. Line up square to the ball and on the imaginary line we discussed earlier. Keep your knees bent and over your toes so your weight is forward. Don't pull back when the ball is struck. You'll lose your balance and possibly miss the ball. Keep that chin over your knees.

Stay confident and keep your eyes on the ball through the entire shot. When the shot is taken, identify the path of the ball and move so the ball travels toward the center of your body. Use your leg pads to block the ball from entering the cage. When the ball hits your pads, give with the shot so it doesn't rebound too far off your pads and into the waiting offense's stick.

Lunge

Sometimes the ball moves so quickly in the circle that you don't have time to center your body with the shot. In these situations, use your leg pads to block the ball.

Rely on your reflexes. Because you are out of line with a direct shot, you've got to spread your body farther than its standard width. Lunge to the ball with the foot that is closest to the shot. If the ball is to your right, lunge with your right foot. Turn your foot and knee away from your body and block the shot with the side or instep of your foot. Try to keep your chin over your knee. Your weight stays forward when your head is forward, giving you better balance and body control. This helps prevent the ball from rebounding wildly off your pads.

Time your lunge so you meet the shot when your foot lands. Don't lift your foot high off the ground, but keep it close to the ground so the ball can't pass under your foot and into the cage.

If the velocity or proximity of the shot doesn't allow you enough time to get your body in front of the ball, lunge to stop the ball with your leg (or foot). Turn your knee and foot outward to make the save.

Split Save

Occasionally, a shot is even wider than your lunge. Desperate times call for desperate measures, so stretch out those legs—especially the groins and hamstrings—and exercise a split.

The actual body positioning of the split save is similar to that of a sprinter clearing a hurdle in the air. The leg that extends in front of you is the one closest to the ball, while the back leg bends and tucks up underneath you.

Once the shot is taken, move toward the ball quickly. Step off your back foot, extend your front leg to the ball, and drop into a split. Bend your back leg and point your knee out to the side. Pull your heel up so it tucks behind your rear

Split saves are a perfect example of why it's so important for goalies to stretch. Failing to get loose before making a save like this can cause injury.

end. Push your head forward over the knee of your extended leg, and if possible, line it up with the shot.

The toes of your front foot point toward the sky. If your right leg is the saving leg, extend your right hand and stick forward along the line of your leg. Hold your stick out as far as you can along the ground so the stick extends beyond your foot. This gives you extra equipment to save the ball. When the left leg is your saving leg, hold your left hand above the left leg, palm facing the ball. This increases the height of your saving capacity on that side. Your other hand stays on the ground in front of your hips and near your tucked back knee.

Attempt to block the shot with the inside of your extended foot. This will redirect the ball in toward your body and reduce the chance of a second (rebound) shot. Once you block the ball, place your hands on the ground on either side of your hips and push up to get your feet under you. Clear the ball away from the dangerous area in front of the cage.

Stick Dive

The stick dive is a lateral dive used when the ball is too far away for you to block it with a body part. Use the stick dive for shots that are to the far right or left of you, to intercept a pass in the circle, or to take the ball away from the shooter when there is no other defense back with you (one-on-one situations). Hold the stick in your right hand with the flat side facing the ball. Use a reverse grip when the ball is on your left side.

From the ready position, take a step toward the ball. Dive off that foot in the direction of the ball so you can intercept it with your stick. Your body faces the ball as you dive so your back is to the cage. In the air, extend your right arm with the flat side of the stick facing the ball. Extend your left arm as well, providing support and height to your block. On the reverse stick dive, place your left hand behind the stick with the palm facing forward for additional support. Keep your head between your arms, and keep your eyes on the ball.

As you land, your outer thigh contacts the ground first, followed by your hip, rib cage, and shoulders. After landing, immediately push up with your hands to stand up, all the while keeping your eyes on the ball and the ball in front of you. Get up and clear the ball out of the circle.

Double Stack Block

The double stack block is a very aggressive block in which the goalie charges the shooter and slides toward her legs first to block the shot.

This is used in a one-on-one situation when the goalie is the only defense back and must attack the attacker to clear the ball out of danger.

As soon as the shooter enters the circle, move directly toward her. By pressuring her aggressively you're forcing her to make a decision with the ball. As she draws her stick to shoot the ball (you should be about two yards from her at this point), slide forward toward her with your leg pads facing her. Keep both legs in front of you and stacked on top of each other. With your pads facing the shooter, you are creating a giant wall that is moving at her. Your pads will block her shot. Slide forward so you meet the ball just as the ball is hit, blocking the shot and sending it away from the shooter. Push up with your upper body to stand and follow your block. Beat the shooter to the ball so you can clear it out of the circle.

Aerial Blocks

When the ball is coming at you through the air, use your glove or stick to block the shot. Let the ball hit your glove or stick so the ball will drop in front of you. You are not permitted to hold or swing at the ball in any way that will propel it forward. This is considered a dangerous play.

If you are saving the ball with your glove and the shot is above your waist, point your left fingers up to the sky. (Remember, your right

Whether the aerial shot is to your left, your right, or directly at you (above and next page), use your glove whenever possible to make the save.

hand is holding the stick.) If the ball is below your waist but still in the air, point your left fingers down when you block it with the glove. If it is on your right side and close to you, reach across your body with your left hand—palm facing forward—to block it. Always keep your palm facing the ball when glove saving. Allow your hand to give with the ball so it drops in front of you. Clear the ball out to the sides and away from the attacking offense.

When the ball is shot high and away from the right side of your body, use your right arm with the stick extended to block the ball. Point the toe up and turn the stick so the flat side faces the ball. To save a high ball with your stick, step onto your right foot and spring into the air with your stick outstretched to meet the ball. Do not swing at the ball and hit it out of your area. Bat the ball downward and let it drop to the ground.

CLEARS

So now you can block the ball . . . but you can't just let it sit at your feet, because hungry offensive players will overtake the ball and score! You've got to quickly clear the ball out of the circle.

When you are clearing, always clear to the closest sideline. Never clear the ball across the cage. It creates a perfect scoring opportunity for the other team. The last thing you want to do is serve up an assist for the opposing team.

The first step to clearing is to judge the speed and distance of the ball and determine the correct timing for the clear. If you see an open teammate off to the side, direct your clear to her and yell her name so

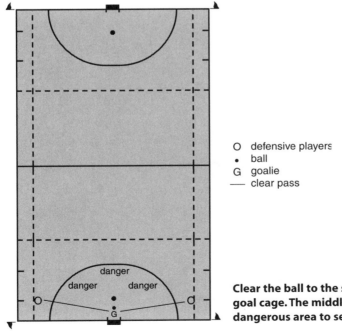

O   defensive players
•   ball
G   goalie
—   clear pass

Clear the ball to the sides from the goal cage. The middle of the field is a dangerous area to send the ball.

she expects the ball. "Goalkeepers can create attacks by clearing it directly to their defenders. They can really help accelerate the transition process," says Coach O'Haire.

Practice clearing the ball with both your left and right feet. One foot will naturally be stronger, so pay extra attention to building strength in your weaker foot. Keep your weight forward when clearing. When your weight goes back on your heels, the ball launches into the air. The ref will whistle a dangerous play and your opponent receives a corner.

Jab Kick

The jab kick is a block and clear in one motion. Use this in fast-paced games, such as those played on Astroturf. Because the ball moves faster on artificial surfaces, the shots coming at you are much harder and have much more speed than those on grass. They are also, however, more predictable due to the smooth surfaces. Adjust to the increased pace of the game and react quickly. Blocking and clearing the ball in one movement maintains the pace of the game.

Stand at the appropriate angle between the cage and the shooter in the ready position. Keep your eyes on the ball through the entire shot and clear. When the ball comes to you, jab the foot that is closest to the ball to meet it. Turn your toes and knee to face away from your body so the inside of your jabbing foot contacts the ball. Keep

Always remember to move out and cut the angle down on the shooter.

your knee bent and your head over your knees so your weight is forward. Square your foot to where you want to clear the ball. Pass to the closest sideline or to an open defender. Keep your palms facing forward and shift your body weight forward through the kick to provide power.

Crossover Jab

The crossover jab is a similar motion from the jab clear, except you clear the ball with the foot opposite of the direction you want the ball to go. To send a ball to the left, cross over and hit it with your right foot. Use the crossover jab to send the ball away from the cage and parallel to the end line.

When the ball comes to you, keep your rear foot on the ground with your weight balanced on the ball of your foot. Your jabbing foot comes out in front of your rear foot so the heel rests ahead of your back foot's toes. Jab the ball with the inside of your foot to kick it to the side. Keep your post leg (nonkicking leg) slightly bent to maintain balance.

Punch Clear

All goalies must learn the punch clear. The punch clear is a foot-first slide tackle in which the goalie uses the sole of her sliding foot to punch the ball away from the dribbler or knock a loose ball out of the circle.

Charge out to the shooter at an angle that narrows her shooting angle. The immediate pressure forces her to do something at your initiation. This can be unnerving for her and even intimidating.

When you come within one to two yards of the ball, slide onto the ground, similar to a foot-first softball slide. Slide with your punching leg closest to the ground so the outside of your ankle and foot are touching the ground. With the punching leg extended, bend your other leg inward as you slide. When you close in on the

The post leg is slightly bent, and your head stays over the ball. Clear the ball with the inside or toe of your foot.

ball, straighten your bottom leg and punch the ball away from the shooter with the sole of your foot. Immediately after punching the ball, find the cleared ball and return to your feet.

Drop Kick and Punt

Just as blocking an aerial shot is different from blocking a ground shot, clearing an aerial shot is slightly different from clearing a ground shot. Two typical aerial clears are the drop kick and the punt. The most important thing to remember when executing these clears is that when sending the ball into the air, you must be sure that it is high enough to clear all players in front of you. It will be called a dangerous play if you direct an aerial clear into an oncoming player—purposely or accidentally.

The quicker and easier of the two clears is the drop kick. Depending on the angle you hit the ball with your foot, this clear can be delivered on the ground or in the air.

As the ball comes at you in the air, you use your glove or stick to block the ball; anticipate where the ball is dropping and move to that spot. As the ball comes down to the ground, pull your kicking leg back and kick your leg forward, extend your knee and foot completely forward, and contact the ball with the inside of your kicking foot. To keep the ball along the ground, lean forward and keep your leg over the ball. Try to contact the top of the ball to keep it low. To clear the ball in the air, lean back and contact the lower half of the ball. Square your hips and shoulders to the target you are aiming your clear to reach. Keep your head steady through the entire process.

The punt is slightly more advanced and requires more time and space to execute. Block an aerial shot with your glove. Extend your glove out in front of you near your waist and drop the ball from your palm. As you drop the ball, step forward with your nonkicking foot. Swing your kicking leg forward and punt the ball out and above all players in the circle. Square your shoulders and hips completely square with your target and extend your kicking foot.

GRACE UNDER FIRE

There are certain pressure situations that all goalies must prepare for. One-on-one play, a fast breakaway, defensive corners, and penalty strokes are examples of these types of intense situations. These are times when you are called upon to perform under pressure and be the heroine of your hockey team. Thriving under pressure and a tremendous amount of confidence are prerequisites for goalkeeping. Just remember, you are part of a team and the goalie is simply the last line of defense. "The goalie doesn't allow a goal to be scored, the entire team allows the goal," says Coach O'Haire. "I tell my players not to worry about mistakes—if a bad goal goes in, there's nothing you can do but move on and get ready for the next play."

ONE ON ONE

As a goalie, you will be confronted with one-on-one situations. This occurs when a player from the other team sprints down the field with the ball on a breakaway and there are no field defenders back except for you.

The most important thing to do in this situation is to stay confident and focused. Do not panic. As you see your opponent coming down the field, prepare to aggressively defend your territory. This is your cage, your goal; you do not welcome any uninvited guests. As she comes tearing into the circle, charge out toward her to cut down her angle. Race out to her and block or tackle the ball away from her. Do not stay back in the cage and wait to block the ball with two feet on the ground. Don't be the hunted. Become the hunter.

Force the dribbler to choose a side. Do not let her stay in the middle of the circle, where the shooting angle for the cage is largest. Usually, goalkeepers like to keep the shooter on their stick side, the dribbler's reverse stick side.

Know that the dribbler will attempt to dodge around you. Be ready to adjust your footwork and react quickly to sudden movements. Execute a stick dive or punch dive to intercept the ball. The bottom line is you must be aggressive and charge the shooter as soon as she enters the circle.

By aggressively coming out to confront the attacker on a breakaway, you take the action to her. It forces her to execute a shot more quickly than she would have liked.

OVERTIME

If at the end of a regulation game there is a tie, the game goes into overtime. The exact breakdown of overtime play varies depending on the level (high school, collegiate, or international) and can also be affected by state rules at the high school level. Generally, at the high school level, a game will go into overtime only if it is a conference or championship game. Otherwise, a tie is an acceptable conclusion to the game. The first phase of overtime is seven a side. Seven players, including the goalie, from each team take the entire field and play for 10 minutes. Regulation rules apply. The first team to score wins. If after 10 minutes no one has scored, there is a five-minute break before another 10-minute game of seven a side. There are no substitutes allowed during play, so any changes must be made during the break.

If after the second seven a side it is still a tie, the game goes to penalty strokes. Each coach chooses five players. The teams alternate shooters, so the goalies are in the cage every other shot against a different stroker from the other team.

CORNER PLAY

During a defensive corner, the goalie has to be focused on the play because the offense heavily outnumbers the defense. When the ref calls a corner, stand in the cage with your toes and stick behind the goal line. Four other defenders are back with you—two outside the cage, closest to the hitter, and two inside the cage with you. The two defenders outside the cage cover the hitter and the shooter (the girl the hitter passes to). Inside the cage, the two other defenders are on either side of you. The one closer to the hitter trails two steps behind the fly. The other one, farthest from the hitter, covers the far post. She takes one step out of the cage and makes sure that no shots enter in that far corner. Make sure you can see the offensive player who is hitting the ball out. If your defenders are in the way, reposition them so you can see the ball.

As soon as the ball is hit, come out of the cage. Follow the ball to the shooter—the girl who receives the hit. Make sure you are at the correct angle to block her shot. Your defensive fly rushes the ball, and your other defenders cover their marks and the post. If the fly does not get the ball away from the shooter, you take the initial shot. This shot is usually taken from the top of the circle.

Keep your eyes on the ball and stay in a ready position. Your weight is forward, your head is over your knees, and you are confident and determined. Once the shot is taken, do whatever you can to block it—whether that's a standard block, a stick dive, or a sliding dive. Stop the shot and clear the ball hard out of the circle, taking the advantage away from the offense. If you cannot see the ball because a defender is in your way, tell her to move! It is important that you are vocal about what you see from your position.

PENALTY STROKE

When the goalie holds, covers up, or somehow protects the ball from the offense, or if another defender uses one of her body parts to stop a shot that would otherwise have been a goal, the ref calls a penalty stroke. A penalty stroke will also be called if the defensive players continuously run off the end line early during penalty corners.

During a stroke, all players stand behind the 25-yard line except for the goalie and one shooter from the offense. The shooter lines up on the stroke line, which is the line seven yards in front of the goal cage. The goalie stands with her heels on the goal line in the ready position.

This is a high-pressure situation, but more pressure is on the shooter to make the shot. As the goalie, stay ready, poised, and relaxed. Your reflexes will guide you on this. There isn't much time for decision making, so trust your gut reaction and keep your eyes on the ball. The shooter is flicking or pushing the ball into the cage. Most of these shots are flicks, so be prepared to stop an aerial shot with your glove or stick.

Stay low in the ready position. A lower center of gravity helps you move in any direction. You can spring up, dive down to the sides, or use your feet to block a shot close to your body.

If the ball is in the top right corner, use your stick. As soon as you stop the ball, the stroke is over; there is no rebound so don't worry about a clear.

ADVICE

As mentioned in this chapter, the goalie is a pressure position. For beginners it can be frustrating because there is so much to learn. But focus on every opportunity you have to play the ball instead of worrying about how many goals or saves you have. "The important things to emphasize," says Coach O'Haire, "are the good things beginners do that stop a shot on goal—or a goal—from happening: a good kick, being ready, communicating with the defenders."

For high school players looking to play in college, focus on becoming a master of the basics. "You have to know, 'My left foot is as strong as my right and my left hand is as strong as my right hand is as strong as my stick,'" says Coach O'Haire. Focus on the basics—blocking, clearing, and communicating.

"At the international and collegiate levels, the opponent has the skill to punish you for a mistake. If you eliminate the mistakes from the get-go, you don't allow them to punish you," he concludes.

DRILLS AND GAMES

Warm Up Your Feet

Players: Goalie
Equipment: Goalie equipment and five balls
Distance: One yard in front of goal cage

Line up five balls one yard in front of the goal cage. Spread out the balls so they are all about one foot apart from each other and parallel to the goal line. Position yourself behind the first ball and work your way down the line, kicking the balls straight into the back of the cage. Move from left to right first, stepping on your right foot and kicking with your left. Practice kicking the ball with your instep and with the toe of your kicker. Step, kick, step, kick, until you reach the last ball. Set the balls up again and work your way back down the line, starting from the right and moving left. Step with your left foot and kick with your right.

Do the Shuffle

Players: Goalie
Equipment: Kickers, leg pads, chest protector, goal cage
Distance: Circle

Start at the center of the goal line in the middle of the cage. Charge out of the cage to the stroke mark as if there was a shooter at the top of the circle and you were coming out to block her angle. When you reach the stroke mark, break down to the ready position. Drop step to the right post and stand up against the post as if you were blocking a shot coming from the right corner of the field. Shuffle along the goal line to the center of the cage and sprint out again to the stroke mark. Drop step to the left post and be in position to block a shot there. Shuffle back to the center of the cage.

Repeat this drill until you cover each post three times. The purpose of this drill is to build up endurance and to warm up your feet and legs. This drill also helps you work on angles and movement in the circle when the opponents move the ball around the circle in front of you.

Partner Up

Players: Two goalies
Equipment: Goalie pads and kickers, one ball
Distance: Up to 10 yards

Stand five yards away from your partner goalie. Kick the ball to her using a jabbing motion, and she will jab the ball back to you. First work on stopping, then on kicking, and gradually work up to kicking the ball back in one motion.

Once your feet are warmed up and your kicking is accurate, each of you take a step back. Continue this until you are 10 yards away from each other, increasing the strength of your kicks as you go. Time yourselves for five minutes and count how many clean kicks you send back and forth to each other. It doesn't count if the kick is off target!

Rapid Fire

Players: Goalie and field players
Equipment: Goalie equipment, stick, balls, and cage
Distance: 16-yard circle

The field players on the team line up around the circle, each with their stick and a ball. The goalie is in the cage. The player on the far left of the circle starts. She drives the ball from the circle line right on cage. The goalie stands in the ready position, angled at the shooter. As soon as the shot is hit, the goalie blocks and clears the ball out of the circle. As soon as the shot is cleared, the next player on the circle takes a shot on the cage. The goalie must quickly clear the ball and reset in the ready position at a new angle to the new shooter to block the next shot. This continues at a fast pace all the way around the circle until every player has taken a shot.

All players collect their balls and set up again around the circle. This time, the shooters alternate sides. The player on the far left goes first. As soon as the goalie blocks and clears her shot, the player on the far right of the circle takes a shot. After her shot, it goes back to the left side, and the next player on that side takes a shot. The goalie must move quickly from one side to the other to block each shot. The last player to go will be in the middle at the top of the circle.

All players collect their balls and set up again around the circle. Just as in the first round, one by one the players take a shot on the goal from the circle line. However, this time they follow their shots. The goalie must quickly block and clear the ball away from the charging shooter, who is going in to collect her rebound. As soon as the goalie clears the ball out of the circle, the play is done and the next player on the circle takes her shot and follows it.

Blocking in Motion

Players: Goalie and one player
Equipment: Goalie equipment, tennis balls, cage, cone
Distance: Circle

Set up one cone opposite the right post and in line with the stroke mark. One field player is standing opposite the left post with a pile of five balls. The goalie starts in position in the center of the cage.

The goalie charges out to the first cone as if it was an offensive player about to shoot. As soon as the goalie reaches the first cone, the player with the ball sets up to take a shot. The goalie must quickly move from the cone to the real shooter and block the ball using a standard block, lunge, split save, or dive. She is focusing on quick footwork to change her angles and quickly get to the shooter. Repeat five times. The shooter changes her shooting angle as the goalie rushes out to the cone so that the goalie doesn't know where the shot is going to come from. Shooters never take a strong drive when they are close to the goalie. If a shooter is at the top of the circle and the goalie is coming out of the cage, driving is permitted. However, work on dodges and ball placement to get around the goalie. This prevents any unnecessary injuries during practice.

Control the Clear

Players: Goalie and one field player
Equipment: Goalie equipment, cage, four cones, five balls
Distance: Circle

Set up two cones on either side of the cage in the circle one yard from the end line. One player stands above the stroke line, near the top of the circle, with a pile of five balls. The goalie is at the center of the cage on the goal line.

The field player pushes a ball strongly to the goalie. The goalie rushes out to the ball and clears the ball to the sides, away from the center of the cage, using the crossover jab. When using the crossover jab, aim to send the ball parallel to the end line and below the cone closest to the end line. Alternate feet.

Collect the balls and set up again. This time, the field player pushes the ball to the corners of the cage. The goalie rushes out and lunges at the ball, sending it away to the closest sideline. Aim for the ball to go between the cones on either side of the circle.

One on One

Players: One and goalie, good for the entire team!
Equipment: Stick, balls, goalie equipment
Distance: 25-yard area

The field players line up on the 25-yard line. One at a time, they have 10 seconds to dribble into the circle and go against the goalie one on one to score. As soon as either the shooter scores or the goalie clears the ball out of the circle, the play is over. Shooters must be quick and focus on getting a good shot off and using a dodge to move around the goalie. Goalies practice coming off the goal line and playing aggressively to cut the shooters' angle down and come up with the ball.

A HEALTH TIP

Remember that you are wearing a lot of protective equipment and it gets hot in there. Take a lot of water breaks when playing—especially when playing in excessive heat!!

8
OFFENSIVE STRATEGY

You know your positions. You know the rules. You can dribble, you can pass, you can shoot, and you can tackle. Now let's talk strategy.

This chapter focuses on offensive team play. Team strategies include cutting, passing and, most important, communicating. You are part of a team, and it takes an entire team to win games. When you reflect on your individual role on the field, acknowledge how that role helps the greater good of the team.

ORGANIZATION

Ask any coach to name the most critical components of team play, and "organization" will spearhead that list. "You need organized movement and teamwork between attacking players to have an effective offensive movement," says Coach Shelton. You need to understand not only your position but every other position on the field as well.

Forwards

The forward line players are the most offensive players on the team. This front line is the first wave of attack, using dodges, passing, and strong stick skills to manipulate and infiltrate the defense. Offensive players have the authority to dictate the game. You're holding the ball and know when you are going to dribble and when (and where) you are going to pass. Use this knowledge to force the defense to react to you.

There's no way around it. To win, you've got to score.

Don't allow them to influence your play. That is the secret to a successful offense.

"One of the great weaknesses in our country is that we don't use enough deception in our offensive game. Work on stick fakes and body fakes and lots of different things to manipulate the defense. I don't think forwards do enough to make the defender do what they want them to. The defense is always trying to manipulate forwards, but I don't think it's in a forward's mindset to manipulate the defender. This deception needs to be taught at early levels," Coach Shelton says.

Forwards are on high alert as soon as the play enters the offensive 25-yard area. Anytime the ball is in this area, there is a chance of scoring. The first thing to do is to push into the circle and pressure the goalie. Keep your stick on the ground at all times in the circle. This allows you to easily deflect the ball into the cage.

When attacking in the circle, the outside wings are in front of the two goalposts. Their primary role is to cover the ground just in front and slightly outside of the goalposts. If a shot is going wide, redirect the shot on goal. If a pass comes on a diagonal across the circle, direct an immediate shot on goal. From this position, you can also follow up rebounds that fall in front of the goalie. The pressure on the goaltender makes it difficult for her to stay calm and

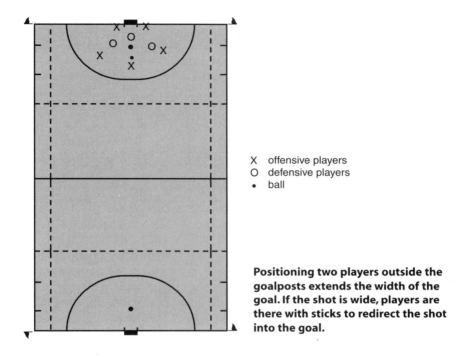

X   offensive players
O   defensive players
•   ball

Positioning two players outside the goalposts extends the width of the goal. If the shot is wide, players are there with sticks to redirect the shot into the goal.

focused. Angle your body so your shoulders are square to the point between the goal cage and the ball. Lead with the foot that is opposite from the side the ball is on (if the ball is on the left side, lead with your right foot). This naturally opens your body up to the ball. As the ball moves around the circle, adjust your positioning accordingly.

The two inside forwards stand in front of the goalie to the left and right of the stroke line with their sticks on the ground. Call for the ball by shouting, "Stroke!" to let your teammates know where you are. The stroke line is one of the highest-scoring areas on the field because it's a prime spot for deflection shots. Another responsibility of the inside forwards is to obstruct the view of the goalie. Roam closely in front of her and put the pressure on. Your harassing ways can lead to goals and rebound opportunities.

The forwards are always working together and talking to each other. Because the circle is a tight space, always call for the ball so two of you aren't going to the ball at the same time. If two players are going for the same ball, the player with the ball on her strong stick side always takes the shot. Still, let your teammate know you're there and in a better position to take the shot.

NCAA DIVISION I CHAMPIONS	
2001	Michigan State University
2000	Old Dominion University
1999	University of Maryland
1998	Old Dominion University
1997	University of North Carolina
1996	University of North Carolina
1995	University of North Carolina
1994	James Madison University
1993	University of Maryland
1992	Old Dominion University

Midfielders

Midfielders are transitional players. They constantly contribute on defense. Midfielders are the second wave of the offensive attack, backing up the forwards and filling in the spaces behind them to give support. The midfielders must stay close to the front line to eliminate gaps that form in the field between the waves of attack.

When attacking in the circle, position yourself around the top of the circle to support the forwards. While the forwards are pressuring the goalie and deflecting the ball, take long shots from the top of the circle, aiming for the corners of the cage. Your shot will either fire into the goal or deflect off a teammate's stick and into the cage. If space in front of the cage is left vacant by a forward, step up and fill that space. Call for the ball as you move in front of the cage. Streaking through the circle stirs things up and confuses the defense.

The circle can become a congested area of attackers and defenders. If you move to an area that's already crowded, you're also bringing your defender into the crowd. Make timely runs into space, but avoid overcrowding an area. Pull out of the circle if it's getting too crowded; backpedal out to a side and your defender will follow you. Then cut around her and back into the circle when you see a space open up. This movement keeps the circle from getting too crowded and too stagnant. Settling into one position gives the defense time to set up and mark you tightly.

Backs

Backs are the third wave of the offensive attack. They push up behind the midfielders, filling in the spaces behind and between them. Just as the midfielders don't want to allow too much space between themselves and the front line, the backs must stay in a close support role behind the mids. As a result, the entire team moves in one single unit.

While the backs' primary responsibility is to defend, there are times when the backs go into attack mode.

Any time the ball enters the circle, push up near the 25-yard line. You are a threatening player because you're the least of the defenses' concern. They are concentrating on marking the forwards and midfielders. But what happens if you shoot into the circle—unguarded—in front of the cage and receive a pass? GOAL!!!

A back shooting into the circle is an effective method of attack. Remember, though, not all backs can shoot through at the same time. Players must stay in position to defend a quick transition.

Diagonals

A general offensive rule is that the lines of players across the field, the forward line, midfield line, and back line, work on diagonals. If the right side has the ball, the line of players moves forward on a diagonal, ending with the left side farthest up the field.

With that rule in mind, you're able to envision where each player is as the ball moves around the field. The advantage to this strategy is that if the ball is hit down the field, you have every offensive player in position to threaten the defense.

As the ball moves around the field, your team constantly readjusts itself. The positions that you take on the field provide the structure for the game, but they are not set in stone.

You are allowed to color outside the lines, but if you are going to move into someone else's space on the field, let them know you're coming. Switching positions occasionally confuses the defense, but don't allow it to confuse your own team.

The left inner and right inner, for example, will often switch sides with each other. If you're playing left inner and dribbling into the right inner's space, call out "switch," so she knows to move out of her area and over to your left side.

	NCAA DIVISION II CHAMPIONS
2001	Bentley College
2000	Lock Haven University
1999	Bloomsburg University
1998	Bloomsburg University
1997	Bloomsburg University
1996	Bloomsburg University
1995	Lock Haven University
1994	Lock Haven University
1993	Bloomsburg University
1992	Lock Haven University

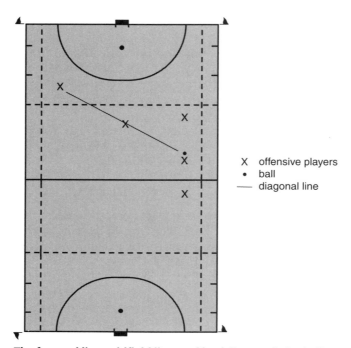

The forward line, midfield line, and back line work the ball toward the goal on diagonals. If the right side has the ball, the farthest point of the diagonal is completely across the field and closest to the offensive end line of the defense. The midfielder may make a short pass to the center of the field, a long pass across the field to the farthest point, or—as a safe alternative when the forward players are closely marked—a short pass backward.

COMMUNICATION

A fundamental element of being organized on the field is communicating with your teammates. Talk to your teammates throughout the game, using quick, decisive language that immediately provides information for your teammates.

Remember, when you are dribbling, keep your eyes on the ball and on the field. There's a lot to look at, but the best players see everything that is happening on the field. Talking to each other helps supplement the dribble with information. Shouting "flat right" tells your teammate that she can pass the ball to the right. When calling for the ball, just make sure you are open and in a position to receive it.

Use that voice box to warn your teammates about incoming defenders and whether or not the dribbler should pass or continue to

If you notice a defender closing in on your teammate, shout "Coming on!" This attacker has heard her teammate's warning and is moving clear of the defender and her outstretched stick.

dribble. Eleven pairs of eyes are better than one, so never hesitate to shout out what you see happening on the field. If you notice a defender closing in on your teammate who is dribbling—even if you are on the other side of the field—shout, "Coming on!" It tells your teammate to pass the ball immediately or risk losing possession. Or perhaps you're the one dribbling the ball and a teammate shouts "Carry!" or "Time!" This lets you know that you have time and space to move the ball.

Nonverbal Communication

Not all communication is verbal. Nonverbal communication techniques include eye contact, head nods, stick pointing—even mind reading. It's not exactly the psychic hot line, but teammates who play together for a long time become familiar with each other's tendencies and actions in certain situations.

An important form of nonverbal communication is eye contact. When you are either passing or receiving the ball, make eye contact with your teammate.

As the hitter, indicate where you want the ball to go with your eyes and your teammate will respond by moving to that space. Head nods can also be used to accomplish this, however, they are more obvious and easily interpreted by the defense.

As a receiver, make eye contact with the hitter so you can anticipate wherever she's sending the ball. You're also telling the passer that you are ready to receive the ball.

Timing

Timing is also a crucial component to nonverbal communication. Sustaining a rhythm with your teammate allows you to anticipate more effectively and provides a distinct advantage over the defense. If you are passing the ball to an open space and have made eye contact with a teammate who is moving to that space, time your hit so that your teammate and the ball arrive in the space at the same time. If she's farther away, delay your hit until she starts to move, and don't hit the ball hard. If she's close to the space, send a crisp pass immediately.

	NCAA DIVISION III CHAMPIONS
2001	State University of New York at Cortland
2000	William Smith College
1999	The College of New Jersey
1998	Middlebury College
1997	William Smith College
1996	The College of New Jersey
1995	Trenton State College (now The College of New Jersey)
1994	SUNY Cortland
1993	SUNY Cortland
1992	William Smith College

MOVING WITH THE BALL

It is a team effort to move the ball down the field. Players must dribble, pass, cut, communicate, and listen. There are 10 other players on the field who are striving to reach the same goal as you are, so use each other to produce. The best way to work the ball down the field is by passing. As mentioned in chapter 4, Passing and Receiving, the ball moves faster than any dribbling player. Passing gets all your teammates involved, while it creates and uses space.

The Through Pass

There are two basic passing patterns used when moving the ball down the field: the through pass and the flat pass. The through pass is a forward pass straight up the field. This is the most aggressive pass because it attacks the defensive territory.

When making a through pass, look up to the teammate who is calling for the ball. Glance around to make sure no defenders will intercept the pass. Pay attention to where the receiver is holding her stick and send a strong hit in front of her stick.

When receiving a through pass, keep your back to the dribbler and look over the shoulder that you are receiving the ball on. As you're running forward, hold your stick in a strong, shake hands dribbling grip with the flat side facing the passer. Point your stick to the spots you want to receive the ball, either to the left or right of your body. Always keep the toe of your stick on the ground. As your teammate delivers a pass, time your run so that you don't have to break stride to receive it. Once it reaches you, accelerate forward with the ball.

Flat Pass

The flat pass is a horizontal pass to a teammate who is moving into position alongside of you. With no forward passing or dribbling options, a flat pass moves the ball away from opponents that are blocking your progress. A teammate to your side (in the flat) may have clear

When receiving a flat pass, face the passer but be ready to advance forward once you've controlled the ball.

passing lanes to advance the ball upfield. To pass left, simply hit the ball off your front foot. The flat side of your stick naturally faces the left, so it's simple to pass the ball in this direction. When passing to the right, move your feet around behind the ball to the left so your shoulders are square with your passing target. Send the ball to the right with your strong stick side. Avoid using the reverse stick to pass. It is not as accurate or reliable as your strong stick side.

Receive a flat pass with the flat side of your stick facing the dribbler. Your stick is naturally positioned this way when you are to the right of the dribbler. Always move toward the ball when receiving a pass. Waiting for the ball leaves you susceptible to an incoming opponent stepping in and intercepting the pass. With two hands on the stick in the shake hands grip, stay low and keep your eyes on the ball as you move toward the pass. Drop your right hand lower on the stick for greater control and let your stick give as you receive the ball.

When receiving a pass to the left of the dribble, wheel your feet around to the right so your shoulders are square to the passer and you are receiving the ball with your strong stick. Collect the ball and go.

As the receiver of a flat pass from either side, imagine there is a line running through the dribbler parallel to the end lines of the field. Stay behind that line when calling for a flat pass. When your dribbling teammate hits you the ball, move onto the ball with speed. Staying behind the line prevents you from getting ahead of the dribbler and, therefore, the ball. If you are too far ahead, either you are forcing your teammate to pass on a diagonal, which is easily intercepted, or you have to move backward to receive the ball.

Moving in Triangles

The dribbler should always have three passing options at any time and any place on the field—a through pass, at least one flat pass, and a back pass. If the defense closes in and eliminates the flat and through passes, the dribbler can send the ball back to her support behind her, who can then look for her own flat pass.

The idea of having at least three options is called moving in triangles. If you are dribbling the ball, you're one point of a triangle. Your teammate in front of you (through pass) is a second point, and the teammate directly to your left (flat pass) is the third point. That's the first triangle. A second triangle is formed with yourself, your through pass, and the flat pass to your right. Add the person behind you for the back pass, and you've got a series of triangles moving down the field. Moving in triangles is ideal because it gives you passing options in practically every situation.

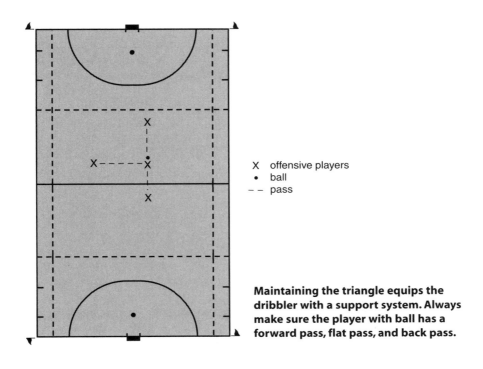

X   offensive players
•   ball
– –   pass

Maintaining the triangle equips the dribbler with a support system. Always make sure the player with ball has a forward pass, flat pass, and back pass.

Two Passes Away

Although we all want to help our teammates, not everyone can be a flat or through pass for the dribbler simultaneously. If too many teammates position themselves in the flat or through spaces, an overcrowded area will result. "One of our key offensive strategies is to spread the field and play the ball wide. When you keep the ball spread, the defense is spread out. The minute you start converging in the middle, it's easier for the defense to defend you," says Coach Morett.

The players closest to the ball assume primary positions of flat and through passes. But that doesn't mean that everyone else sits back and watches the game go by. What happens if the dribbler makes a flat pass? The teammate she passed to now needs her own triangle support. These roles constantly change as the ball moves around the field. Anticipate the progress on the field and prepare to receive the ball in two or three passes from the dribbler. A team that sees passes in advance and stays spread out can wreak havoc on an opponent.

Switching Fields

The field hockey field is 100 yards long and 60 yards wide. Your team is spread out across that field and uses all that space to its advantage.

A good team never uses the same side of the field all the time but rather constantly moves the ball back and forth across the field, all the while moving toward the goal. Moving the ball around the field forces the defense to constantly adjust and readjust. They can never set on a mark or specific area of the field.

Switching fields literally means sending the ball from one side of the field to the other. You can switch fields through a series of small passes or by sending one strong hit all the way across the field to an open teammate. Players in the middle lane of the field—the inners, center mid, and center back—are always thinking about switching fields. They are the link between the left and the right sides of the field. A center player who receives the ball from an overworked right side of the field immediately looks to send the ball to the left side.

PASSING DISTANCES

With a lot of room in the midfield area, your passes are usually 10 yards long or longer. There is more room in this area of the field and therefore more open spaces to pass to. The midfield is also the area where players switch the field of play, which happens often by long passes across the field.

With limited space in the offensive 25, the passing distance narrows to five or 10 yards. With increased defensive pressure, longer passes are more likely to be intercepted.

In the defensive 25, your passes are five yards long, if you pass at all. Your best bet is to send the ball out toward the sides of field and up beyond the 25-yard line. This is not exactly a pass, but it is often referred to as a clear.

Give-and-Go

The most simple and successful passing play is the give-and-go. It is a two-player technique that can be used anywhere on the field. The beauty of this passing combination is that two players work together to beat the defense.

Player 1 dribbles down the field, and Player 2 moves along with her to the right, no more than five yards away. A defender steps up and pressures the dribbler.

Player 1 passes the ball to the right, the defender's nonstick side, where Player 2 is waiting. After passing the ball, Player 1 cuts around the defender to the left and behind her, where she is ready to receive the ball back again from Player 2. As soon as Player 2 receives the ball, she quickly sends it behind the defender to the space where Player 1 is cutting.

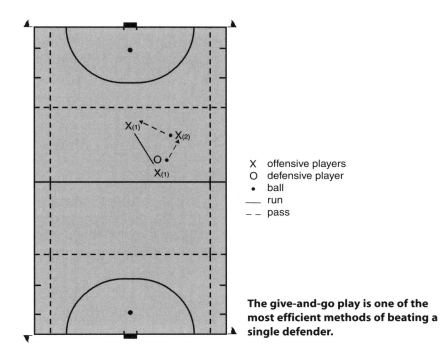

X   offensive players
O   defensive player
•   ball
___   run
_ _   pass

The give-and-go play is one of the most efficient methods of beating a single defender.

When you are Player 2, visualize where you are going to send the ball before receiving it so your execution is immediate. Don't hold on to the ball or the play will be lost because the defender will have the additional time to react to what you're doing. By moving quickly, the defender is defenseless.

Working the Right Side of the Field

The most common strategy for moving the ball down the field is to work it down the right side. This is easier for offense because you are carrying the ball on your strong stick side and the sideline offers protection from an extra line of defense. In addition, defenders have a disadvantage by having to defend you on their nonstick side. They either have to use their reverse sticks, which is more difficult and more likely to result in a foul, or they have to get their feet around, which takes up precious time. Either way, it's a tough assignment for them to defend.

It is also easier to send a drive into the circle and across the cage from the right side of the field. You don't have to move your feet around, as you do when hitting the ball across the circle from the left side, and you can send a strong drive without coming out of your dribble. The forward line is positioned in the circle with their sticks down to deflect the ball into the cage. "One of our big things is to get the ball down the right side along the end line and attack the right offensive corner. We get the defense turned around and bring the ball right into the circle," says Coach Morett.

CUTTING

Cutting creates movement on the field, and movement confuses the defense. Never stand still on the field—cut to receive the ball, cut into a space where you can receive a future pass, or cut out of a crowded area to create more room for your teammates to work. Even if you cut and make a run but never receive the ball, you're still contributing to the offensive attack. By drawing a defender with you, you're creating space for someone else. Also, you'll draw attention from the opposition, which may allow one of your teammates to break free and receive the ball.

Blind Side Cut

A blind side cut is when you cut behind a defender. You move into her blind spot so she can't see where you're going. Don't blow your cover

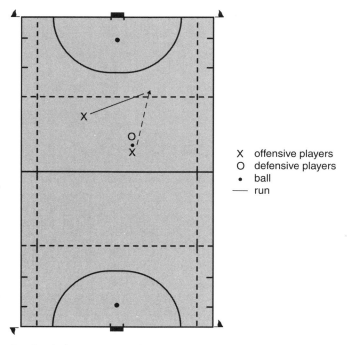

Cutting in between passing lanes blocked by defenders provides an opportunity for the dribbler to pass you the ball. A stationary receiver is much easier to cover than one who is in motion.

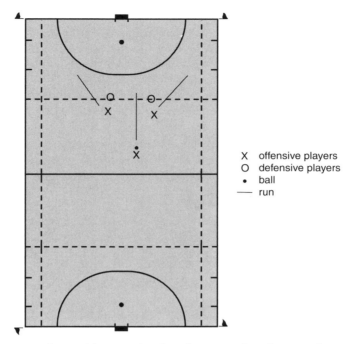

X   offensive players
O   defensive players
•   ball
—— run

Split diagonal cuts not only provide an option for a long pass, but they can also clear space for the dribbler to advance forward. The cutting attackers will draw the attention of the defenders, thus opening up the middle of the field.

by calling verbally for the ball. Instead, use nonverbal signals to indicate your destination and where you want the ball.

Split Diagonal Cut

The split diagonal cut is executed with two teammates. Imagine that the left and right inners are ahead of the dribbler. Each inner makes a simultaneous run. The left inner sprints on a forward diagonal toward the left, and the right inner does the same toward the right. This movement opens up the middle of the field. It also moves the forwards ahead and puts them closer to the cage for a possible scoring opportunity.

FREE HITS AND SIDE INS

Part of a solid offensive strategy is taking advantage of free hits and side ins. Whenever the opposing team is called for a foul, your team gets a free hit. When the other team hits the ball out of bounds along a sideline, your team gets a side in. The ball is placed on the ground where the foul occurred or on the sideline where it was called out of bounds. The ball must be completely still before the hit is taken; if it is moving, settle it with your stick or hand. You must drive or push the ball; lifting it in the air from a free hit or side in is illegal.

To capitalize on free hits and side ins, take them quickly. The more time you take, the more time the defense has to set up around you. The player closest to the ball takes the hit.

The second step to capitalizing on these hits is to be attentive. All players must be five yards from the hitter. If you are hitting the ball and a teammate is standing within five yards of you, tell her to move before you hit it. If she fails to move, the ref will call a foul and award your opponent a free hit.

As the hitter, you cannot touch the ball a second time until another player has contacted the ball. If you are attempting to send a long drive to a teammate but butcher the shot and send the ball only a few inches, back up and allow one of your teammates to run onto the ball. As soon as another stick touches it, it's fair game.

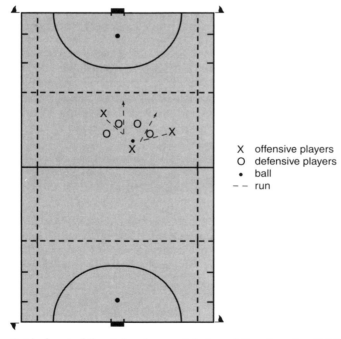

X offensive players
O defensive players
• ball
− − run

Cut in front of the defensive semicircle and then burst upfield in between the lanes created by the defenders. This gives you momentum to run onto a pass, and also may distract the defensive players from blocking the hit.

The defense will set up a ring around the hitter during free hits and side ins. As the hitter, look for a way to penetrate that ring. Just as in any other offensive play, the hitter has flat, through, and back passing options. Offensive players are also cutting into the ring of defenders to create space. If there are no holes to send the ball through, and if all your passing options are blocked, hit it at one of the cutters.

Breaking Up the Defense

As a cutter, always keep your stick on the ground and two hands on your stick. Cut into the defensive ring, move in front of a defender, and dart back out of the ring again. For a moment, you will cross in front of the defender's vision and cause her to lose sight of the ball. This gives the hitter an opportunity to send the ball past that defender. In addition, your movement causes the defenders to move and creates a space for the ball to travel through.

Never stop moving when you cut through the ring of defenders. If you stop in the middle of your run, you're adding to the clutter and failing to create a space. If you stop in front of a defender, you will be called for obstruction, which will result in a free hit for the other team.

As you cut, communicate nonverbally with the hitter. Make eye contact with the hitter and pay attention to where she is hitting the ball. If there is no hole in the ring, the hitter will hit the ball at you. Get your stick on the ball to redirect it through the defense. If you can't get your stick on the ball, simply jump over the ball and let it pass beneath your feet into the area beyond the defense.

LONG HITS

When the defensive team hits the ball out of bounds over its own end line, the offensive team gets a long hit. The wing or midfielder on the side of the field where the ball was hit out takes the long hit. Place the ball on the sideline hash mark five yards from the end line. Attempt to send a strong hit into the circle in front of the goal cage. With your teammates cutting into the circle, anything can happen with a ball in front of the goal.

If the wing is taking the free hit, the midfielder is five yards away and slightly back toward the 25-yard line. She acts as a short back pass. If the defense is tight in the circle, the hitter uses this short pass and the midfielder sends the ball into the circle from a different angle. A second option is that after the short pass is made, the midfielder sends the ball back to the forward who carries the ball toward the circle.

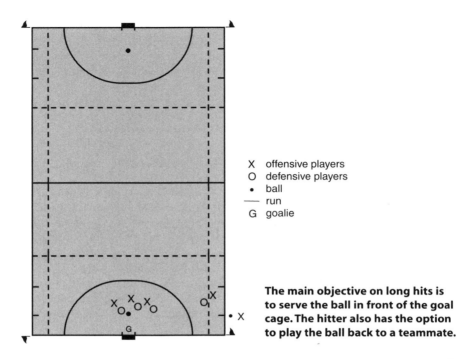

X offensive players
O defensive players
• ball
— run
G goalie

The main objective on long hits is to serve the ball in front of the goal cage. The hitter also has the option to play the ball back to a teammate.

PENALTY CORNERS

The greatest offensive advantage in the game is a penalty corner. When the defense commits a foul in the circle, the offensive team receives a penalty corner. The defense is allowed only four defenders and the goalie during a penalty corner, while the rest of the defensive team retreats to the 50-yard line. They must stay there until the corner play is initiated.

The offensive team sets up with four to six players spread around the circle, and one player who hits the ball into play from the end line. One offensive player is backing up those on the circle. At least two backs are slightly above the 50-yard line.

The offensive hitter stands with the ball on the end line at the hash mark 10 yards from the goalpost. The hit in can be taken from either side of the cage. (There is a hash mark on both sides.) The hitter is usually a forward.

The remaining forwards and one or two midfielders position themselves around the circle, with their sticks and feet outside the circle line. One offensive player is across from the hitter. Two players are at the top of the circle, opposite each of the goalposts. A fourth player is on the opposite side of the circle from where the first player is positioned.

When all the players are set up for a corner and the rest of the defensive team is back on the 50, the ref will blow the whistle. The hitter cannot strike the ball into play until the ref blows the whistle. The defense behind the end line is not permitted to move onto the field until the ball is hit.

The hitter pushes or drives the ball to any of her teammates on the circle. (It is illegal to use an aerial pass at the start of a corner.) Generally, the ball is sent to the top of the circle to the player standing opposite the nearest goalpost to the hitter. This player is usually the one who possesses the strongest shot on the team.

The defense is positioned with sticks and feet behind the end line. The goalie is in the cage with two of the defenders. The other two defenders are standing outside the cage on the side of the hitter. Once the ball is hit, one defender chases the hit and pressures the receiver.

When the ball is hit, the midfielder moves behind the receiver. The receiver must stop the ball completely outside the circle and immediately shoot it on cage. The other forwards, including the forward who hit the ball into play, rush into the circle covering the posts and the area in front of the goalie. The hitter covers the post nearest to her. The player on the opposite side of the circle covers the opposite post.

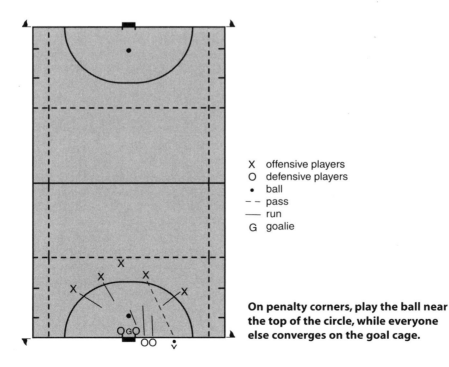

X   offensive players
O   defensive players
•   ball
– –   pass
——   run
G   goalie

On penalty corners, play the ball near the top of the circle, while everyone else converges on the goal cage.

With defensive players charging at you, it's important to control the ball immediately and quickly send a ball at the cage.

This leaves two teammates to rush into the center of the circle near the stroke line. Their job is to get their sticks on the ball, distort defensive players' vision of the ball, and pick up any rebounds from the goalie. The remaining players in the circle stay near the top to avoid crowding in front of the cage. They push the ball back in the circle as it's cleared out.

DRILLS AND GAMES

6v4 Plus Goalie

Players: Six offense, four defense, one goalie
Equipment: Sticks, ball, goalie equipment, cage
Distance: 50 yards (half the field)

Four forwards and two links line up in positions at the 50-yard line. The forwards are slightly ahead of the 50 and the mids behind them. Three backs and a sweeper set up in the defensive end behind the 25 so the two teams are facing each other. One defender hits the ball out from the 16-yard line.

The offensive player closest to where the ball is hit stops it, and the six offensive players move down the field. The offense passes flat and through to work the ball into the circle and around the defense. Practice switching fields and give-and-go passing combinations. Communication is essential. Practice working the ball down the sideline and sending a hit across the circle to be deflected into the goal by teammates. Cut around the defense to create space for a pass or a dribbling option for your teammates.

When you enter the circle, sticks are on the ground. The front line players must remember to cover the goalposts and the stroke area in the circle. Pressure the goalie and pick up her rebounds. Constant communication is the only way to ensure you don't get in each other's way in the circle!

Timing

Players: Two
Equipment: Six balls, three cones
Distance: Five-yard grid

Set up three cones in a triangle with each cone five yards apart. Player 1 stands with a pile of balls five yards away from the top of the triangle. Player 2 starts at one of the cones on the base of the triangle.

Player 2 cuts hard toward Player 1 and the top cone, making eye contact and calling for the ball with her stick on the ground indicating where she wants to receive the pass. Player 2 cuts to the top cone and around it. She should receive the pass as she moves around the top cone so she can carry the ball with her toward the third cone. Player 1 should pass the ball slightly ahead of Player 2 so she can move onto the ball and collect and control it with speed.

This drill mimics cutting situations during free hits. Player 2 is the offense cutting in to break up the defenders—in this case the cones. Timing and communication are essential.

Blindfold Time

Players: Two
Equipment: Stick and ball, cones, blindfold
Distance: 10 yards

Partner up with a teammate. Place a blindfold on your partner. Once you are sure she can't see anything, set up a line of cones two yards apart from each other for your partner to dribble through. Place her at the first cone with her stick and a ball. Move to the end of the line of cones and stand five yards away from the last cone. Direct your partner through the cones by communicating with her. Tell her to dribble left, right, or forward. Tell her if she missed a cone and has to pull back. Practice speaking clearly and directly to your teammates. Your partner should weave through the cones without any problems because of your instructions.

When she reaches the last cone, call for a pass. Be specific about where you are by calling flat to the right or left, or through.

Goals Galore

Players: 10
Equipment: Cones, sticks, ball
Distance: 20-yard square

Mark off a 20-yard square on the field with cones. Set up a goal (using two cones) on the middle of and four yards inside each sideline of the square, four goals total. The goals are four yards wide.

Divide the players so five are on each team and spread out across the grid. The two teams set up to play each other in the grid. Regular field hockey rules apply.

Your team can score at any goal, however to score you must dribble the ball—using a controlled dribble—through the goal or pass the ball through the goal to your teammate on the other side. Keep track of your points!

Circuit Game

Players: Five and goalie, good for the entire team
Equipment: Stick, balls, three cones, cage
Distance: 50 yards

Form five lines around the field. Three are on the 50-yard line at the left, center, and right. The other two are across from each other on the left and right sides of the field near the sidelines on the 30-yard line. Next to the 30-yard line on the left side of the field, set up three cones one yard from each other in a line down the field.

The players at the start of each line work together. The first player at the center of the field on the 50 starts with the ball and sends a strong flat pass to the player to her left on the 50. This left wing passes the ball through to the player at the 30-yard line who is waiting in front of the cones. She cuts back to receive the ball and turns with it toward the cones, dribbling through the cones. When she comes out at the end of the cones, she turns around and passes the ball back to the left wing, where it came from.

The left wing cuts toward the ball to receive it and sends a pass back to the player at the center of the 50-yard line who originally passed her the ball. This center receives the ball and pulls it across to her right side, shifts her positioning, and sends a flat pass to the player at the right on the 50.

The right wing receives the pass and sends a through ball to the player in front of her at the 30-yard line, who cuts back to receive the ball, dribbles down into the right corner of the field, and sends a flat ball across the circle in front of the cage.

As soon as the center passes to the right wing, the center, left wing, and player on the left at the 30-yard line who dribbled through the cones sprint in to the circle and set up in front of the cage for a deflection. They should arrive in the circle just as the right forward player sends the ball across the cage.

One Touch

Players: 10
Equipment: Two goal cages (or four cones), stick, ball
Distance: 25-yard width, 60 length

Place a goal cage in the middle of each sideline between the 25- and 50-yard lines. Set up two teams of five to scrimmage each other within this area, battling the width of the field. Players can only touch the ball one time—they must receive and pass immediately. If you dribble the ball, the other team gets a free hit. Regular field hockey rules apply. Focus on give-and-go, cutting into space, and other passing and movement techniques discussed in this chapter.
Coach's Tip: To increase difficulty, decrease the area of play. To decrease difficulty, increase the area of play.

Give-and-Go

Players: Two
Equipment: Three cones, stick, ball
Distance: 30 yards

Set up three cones 10 yards from each other. These cones represent the defense. One player has the ball, and her partner is to the right of her, about two yards away. The player with the ball dribbles to the first cones and passes to the partner, who is moving with the dribbler. After passing, the dribbler cuts to the left side around the cone (the defender) to receive the pass back. Collect the ball and move to the next cone. Repeat this at every cone. Turn around and go back down the field, switching roles so each player has a chance to be in primary and support roles.

Sideline Support

Players: Team
Equipment: Four cones, stick, ball
Distance: 25 yards wide, 60 length

Set up a goal on each sideline by placing the cones four yards apart. Center the goals between the 25- and 50-yard lines. Two attack and two defense players face each other in the middle of this area, battling the width of the field. The rest of the team divides in half, and each group stands out on one sideline. The teams in the center play each other. Regular hockey rules apply. The sideline players are the support for whichever team has possession. Use them for quick give-and-go passes and offensive support. To score, control dribble or pass the ball through the cones to a teammate. Play for five minutes and switch.

9

DEFENSIVE STRATEGY

Team defense begins with discipline, patience, determination, and communication. "Communication and organization are absolutely paramount," says Coach Shelton. Defense happens everywhere on the field—from your offensive 25-yard area to the transitional midfield area of the field near the 50-yard line. But once the ball enters your defensive 25-yard zone, things really begin to pick up. Defense is not limited to sweepers and backs—all players, forwards and midfielders alike contribute to team defense and must understand what is expected of them during defensive play. This chapter covers basic defensive strategy for all areas of the field. "Preparation and anticipation and having a strong presence are key to strong team defense," says Coach Northcroft. So let's get prepared.

COMMUNICATION

According to Coach Morett, team defense is "all about communication." To play solid defense, you must have the support of your teammates, and it is impossible to support your teammates without communication.

Every defender on your team wants to get the ball and send it out of the backfield definitively. But you can't all be moving to the ball at the same time. "It's important that you have that communication, so you can tell your teammate that she should take the ball, or stay on her girl and you'll take the ball. You can't have two players running in to do the same thing. That's when defensive breakdowns occur," says Coach Morett.

Playing good defense entails more than individual defensive skills. You must function as a cohesive defensive unit.

Key communication terms include, "pressure," "cover," "I got ball," and "mark up." These terms will be explained throughout this chapter. Communication on the field is loud, to the point, and ongoing throughout the game.

MARKING

The most intense defensive situations occur in the defensive 25-yard area and striking circle. The key component to solid defense in these tight situations is solid marking. Marking is another term for one-on-one guarding, or defending. This is similar to man-to-man defense in basketball. Everything in defense stems from good marking. Once the ball enters your defensive 25-yard area, everyone *MUST* mark up. When marking, always keep your girl in front of you and position yourself so you are closer to the ball. Don't let her cut around you and move into the space behind you unguarded. This is a defender's nightmare.

Bend deep at your knees and stay in a low defensive position poised on the balls of your feet, ready to move in any direction. Always keep your opponent in front of you and your stick on the ground. Keep two hands on your stick. Square your shoulders to your opponent and position yourself no more than one arm's length away from her. The closer you are to your defensive goal, the tighter you mark your girl.

Allow some room between you and your opponent so you can read her and react to her movements. Keep your eyes on your opponent's belly button. She will be using quick footwork and body fakes to fool you, but her midsection never lies. Stay focused on her midsection and where the ball is.

Ball Side/Goal Side

When you are marking in the circle you are ball side and goal side. Ball side means that you are on the side of your opponent where the ball is. If the ball is to your left, then you are slightly to the left of her. By positioning yourself ball side, you are closer to the ball than your opponent. That means you have a step on her and can get to the ball quicker, which, according to Coach Northcroft, is key to strong

Even when your mark doesn't have the ball, it's important to stay with her.

defense. "Basically, you've got to beat your player to the ball and not let her get it." Goal side means you are between your girl and the goal cage with your back to the cage and your mark in front of you.

Lower your center of gravity (body position) to prevent your opponent from moving onto the cage. If she attempts to cut around you, stay low and use defensive footwork techniques such as sliding and drop stepping to stay with her and keep her in front of you.

A good defender never sees her goalie blocking and clearing shots. If you are facing the goal cage and watching the goalie in action, then you are out of position. Either you are ignoring your mark and turning your back to her (which means you are obstructing her in the circle, resulting in an offensive corner) or she has cut around you and is now in front of the cage unguarded.

Clearing to the Sides

When you gain possession of the ball, send it out of the circle toward the closest sideline. There is no time to dribble the ball or dodge an opponent in the circle. Never send the ball across the circle. Your opponent may intercept and shoot or deflect the ball into the cage. Always send the ball out and up toward the 25-yard line,

Never turn your back on your mark.

where your forward wings are waiting to receive the ball and continue the offensive transition.

POSITIONING

Part of a strong defense is organization and understanding every player's role on the field. Just as the forwards lead the offensive attack, the backs and sweeper lead the defensive attack. And midfielders are incredibly important to both the offense and defense and must excel at each facet of the game.

Goalie and Sweeper

The goalie and sweeper are the eyes and ears of the defense. Because they are positioned in the center of the field, they have the best view of what is happening and can see when a player from the other team is threatening. The sweeper and goalie work in tandem to eliminate scoring possibilities by directing the defense to cover all dangerous players and spaces. The sweeper and goalie call out the numbers of unmarked players in the circle and alert any defenders who aren't marking up to immediately cover a player roaming free.

The sweeper and goalie are also the only two defensive players who do not mark players from the other team. The goalie always follows the ball and positions herself accordingly to block a shot. The sweeper must be available to cover dangerous spaces in front of the cage and pick up any opponents who move into the circle unguarded. Without a mark, the sweeper has a better view of what is happening on the field and can communicate with her defenders if she sees danger lurking. If everyone on defense is marking up and there is an offensive player unmarked in front of the cage, the sweeper must mark her until another defender recovers. It is always the primary job of any defender to cover an unmarked player in a threatening position.

Backs

The backs are *always* marking up on the field. The typical matchup is that the backs mark the other team's forwards opposite them. For example, the right back is marking the opposing team's left wing. You may be playing a team that has four forwards, while your team has only three backs. In this situation, one midfielder must also mark a forward.

When first taking your positions at the beginning of the game, take note of which player you'll be marking. Take notice of her number and any other defining characteristics—a bow in her hair, for example. These things help you identify her when the ball comes into your defensive end. Call out the number of your mark. Not only does this clarify each defender's responsibility, but it can also intimidate the other team. Continue this type of communication throughout the game.

The backs are the defensive unit of the team. Their priority is to pick up the most dangerous players when the ball enters the defensive zone. If your player with the big bow in her hair is not a scoring threat, pick up an unmarked player who is and call out to your teammates to let them know what you're doing.

Forwards always attempt to get in front of the goalie to obstruct her view and keep the pressure on. As a defender, protect your goalie from attackers. Maintain a low center of gravity to stay balanced and sturdy in your stance. Keep your mark in front of you at all times. Don't let her push you over or move through you. Stay strong and hold your ground. Drop step or shuffle to stay with her and keep her in front of you. And remember, keep your stick on the ground in the circle.

Midfielders

Midfielders have a monumental task in assuming responsibility for both offensive and defensive plays. They are the key transition players. This requires midfielders to be in excellent condition, able to sprint up and down the field throughout the entire game. They must move forward with the offense but be able to recover quickly to assist on defense.

All midfielders mark up when the ball comes into the defensive 25-yard area. They mark the opposing team's midfielders or forwards, if necessary. If you're playing on the right, mark the other team's left midfielder. In the defensive 25, midfielders stay tight on their mark just like the backs. Follow your opponent everywhere in the defensive 25, but always cover the most dangerous player first—even if she's not your girl.

Forwards

Forwards, too, must come back on defense to mark up. Forwards pick up any unmarked midfielders or backs from the other team. Defensive players often make attacking runs out of the backfield. They are just as potentially dangerous as a forward if left open. As a forward, it's sometimes easy to think your only job is to work on offense and score a goal. This is simply not true. Get back and help your team protect the cage.

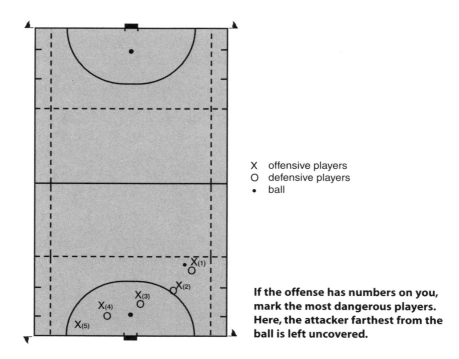

X   offensive players
O   defensive players
•   ball

If the offense has numbers on you, mark the most dangerous players. Here, the attacker farthest from the ball is left uncovered.

Within the defensive 25, always stay on your mark. If there is no one left to mark, take over a dangerous space outside the circle. Work with your team to keep pressure on the dribbler and get the ball from her. When your defense intercepts the ball, move forward toward the 25-yard line to transition to offense. Remember that your defense is sending the ball up to the 25 and out toward the sideline. As soon as you see a defender come up with the ball, take off to present them with an option to deliver a pass.

THE MOST DANGEROUS AREAS

It is not likely that you will be in a situation where every defender has one offensive player to mark and no one is left over. More likely, there will be more offensive players in your backfield than defenders. In this situation, play smart and cover the most dangerous players and/or spaces first. When you are in front of the goal cage, the most dangerous players are the ones in front of the goalie and closest to the ball.

If the ball is on the far right side of the field and there are two unmarked players on the center and left areas of the circle, mark the player closest to the ball—in this case the one in the center of the circle—leaving the one on the left open. If the ball moves to the left side of the field, the entire defensive team shifts so that now the only player not marked is the offensive player on the far right side of the circle.

TRANSITION

Defense doesn't start when the ball enters the striking circle. Your team shifts into defensive mode as soon as the other team gains possession of the ball. Every single player on the field must immediately think defensively and work together to stop the other team from gaining ground and entering your defensive 25-yard area—the danger zone. If some players are still thinking offense, opposing players will be left unmarked and pose threats.

The First Defender

When the other team gains possession of the ball, the player on your team closest to the ball becomes the first line of defense against the opponent. This player assumes the pressure position since she is applying immediate pressure to the ball. When you are the player closest to the ball in this situation, pressure the dribbler by moving in on her in a low defensive position with your stick on the ground and two hands on your stick. As discussed in chapter 6, Tackling, take on a defensive position with a lead foot opposite the direction in which you force your opponent. Force the dribbler away from the middle of the field and toward the nearest sideline. Keep your back toward the goal and angle your body toward the inside of the field. Move with the dribbler and jab or block tackle the ball away from her to stop her from moving forward into an open space. At the very least, your job is to slow down play. This allows your teammates to mark up and get into their defensive position.

Second Defenders

The second wave of defense is the set of players closest to the ball who cover the attackers on the side and forward passing positions and the spaces around them. These defenders are positioned about five to 10 yards from the primary defender. The secondary defenders are responsible for preventing the ball from moving ahead to open spaces and/or players. Eliminate these dangerous passing options. If the dribbler attempts to pass the ball, move toward it to intercept. Remember Coach

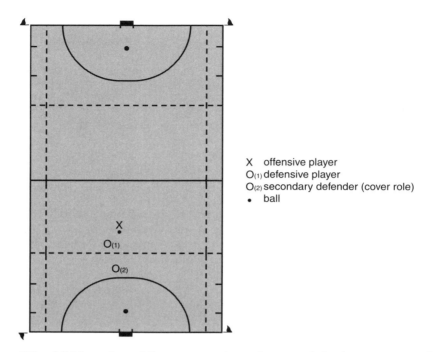

X   offensive player
O(1) defensive player
O(2) secondary defender (cover role)
•   ball

If the dribbler gets past the pressure player, the cover defender steps up to play the dribbler. The original pressure player sprints past and around the play to become the new cover player.

Northcroft's advice to beat your player to the ball. Stay poised in a defensive stance on the balls of your feet and be ready to move in any direction.

The secondary defender in the space behind the primary defender is also known as the cover role. This cover role has a better view of what is happening on the field and can direct the pressure defender to force to the left or right.

Third Defenders

The third wave of defense fans out about seven to 10 yards behind the second wave in the spaces behind and between them. They cover open spaces and offensive players who are positioning themselves two or three passes away from the ball.

The third wave of defense has more space to cover and must be aware of the opposing team's players who aren't directly near the ball. As the ball moves closer to you in this third wave position, you can pinpoint what space around you is the most critical to cover, as well as which players are to be eliminated passing options. Don't worry so much about a back pass, for example, but concentrate on blocking a through pass instead.

As the offensive team moves the ball around the field, these defensive roles will change. If the other team sends the ball across the field, a defender who was once in a third wave position may take the role of the primary defender and pressure the dribbler.

Diagonals

To better understand how the first, second, and third waves of defense are positioned on the field, think about it in terms of diagonals. Just as the offense has a guideline to play on diagonals moving forward down the field, the defense has a diagonal guideline also. The rule, however, is the direct opposite of the rule for offensive strategy. The farther away you are from the ball, the deeper you are in your defensive end. If you're playing left mid, for example, and the right mid is in the primary defensive role, you're probably in a third wave defensive position. In this role, you're stationed diagonally behind where the ball is being played. If the ball moves over to your side of the field, step up into the primary defensive role and pressure the ball. The right mid drops back and is on a diagonal back from the ball and deeper in the defensive zone.

As you fall back on the diagonals, look for dangerous spaces and players in your area. Step into those spaces or near those players to eliminate them as passing options from the dribbler. Although your team always wants to stay spread out on the field, you must be close enough to your teammates to offer support.

Pressure/Cover

"The key to defensive strategy," says Coach Shelton, "is understanding the game in terms of pressuring the ball and reading space and dangerous situations." Pressure/cover is a defensive positioning situation between the first defender and the secondary defender, in the support role behind her. The first defender is the pressure position, and the secondary defender is in the cover role. The cover role player can see what is happening on the field and directs the pressure to force the dribbler right or left. "The cover really needs to direct the play around the ball—generally the person behind the ball has a better vision of how the opposite team is attacking," says Coach Morett. The pressure role has to trust that the cover role is directing her correctly.

The cover role backs up the pressure player. If the dribbler succeeds in moving past the pressure player, the cover defender steps up to the ball. As she does, she calls out, "Ball!" or "Pressure!" to let her teammate know she is moving onto the ball.

The pressure player drops out of the play and moves behind the cover role who is stepping up to the dribbler. When dropping back, always move around the play. If you attempt to run through the middle of the play you will cut your own teammate off and interfere with the dribbler—which is a third party obstruction. A penalty will be whistled. As you run back, stay on the inside of the field, keeping the play toward the sideline. Retreat until you are about five yards behind your teammate and in a cover position. The two positions switch so that the pressure is now cover and the cover now the pressure.

Recovery

Recovery is an essential part of defensive transition. What distinguishes good defenders from the best defenders is their ability to recover quickly. Whenever the other team gains possession and begins moving the ball downfield, your entire team—especially those closest to the play—recovers back to the defensive end to mark up.

Run straight back toward the goal and mark the most dangerous players first. If no one recovered back on the field, the dribbler could

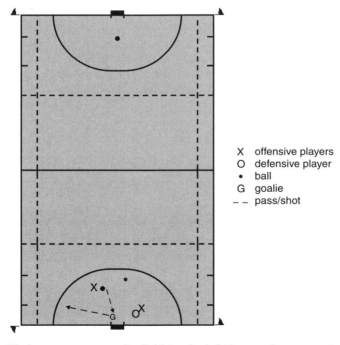

X   offensive players
O   defensive player
•   ball
G   goalie
– –   pass/shot

Hitting a pass across the field (to the left) is very dangerous. Look for an opening on the same side of the field. Keeping the ball out of the middle of the field protects your team from a quick, offensive attack.

just dodge one player and continue unobstructed to the goal. Once you're beat, turn around and sprint back toward your defensive end.

SWEEPER TIME

Sweepers must always play smart and think defensively. As the sweeper, you are the last field defender before the goal. Because you are the deepest defender, you are often confronted with a two-versus-one situation in which two offenders are moving the ball down the field and you are the only defender back (plus the goalie).

To combat this situation, always keep both players in front of you. One player has the ball and is dribbling. The other is probably moving into a forward through spot on one side of you. Stay as deep as the most forward opponent, in front of the dribbler. If possible, contain them on the same side so they don't have the advantage of the entire width of the field. As these two players approach the defensive 25-yard area, maintain your positioning. Stay patient and don't commit to one or the other. When they enter the circle, mark off the second offender without the ball if she is in a threatening scoring position. By marking her out of the play, you are eliminating her from any passing options in the circle. Let the goalie come out and take the dribbler's shot. Two players passing in front of the goalie have a better chance of scoring than one player does. A quick pass forces the goalie to change her angles and makes it more difficult for her to block a shot. That said, always communicate with your goalie during these situations so that she knows what you are going to do.

16-YARD HITS

When the offensive team fouls in the circle or hits the ball off the end line, the defense takes a 16-yard hit out opposite where the foul occurred. If, for example, the foul occurred in the middle of the circle, the hit out is directly at the top of the circle. The 16-yard line is not painted on the field, but crosses through the top of the circle and runs parallel to the end line.

Because the 16-yard hit occurs so deep in the defensive end of the field, treat it as a defensive play despite the fact that your team has the ball. The defender with the strongest drive takes the hits out at the 16-yard line. This is usually a sweeper or center back. However, it can be any defensive player. The quicker you take the hit, the better, because the other team has less time to set up. In 16-yard hits, look for big through passes up the field or small flat passes toward the sideline. Never hit the ball across the center of the field. If the hit is on the left side of the field, only look to send the ball up the left side. Crossing it to the right is too risky. It can be intercepted by the other team and create a goal scoring opportunity.

FREE HITS AND SIDE INS

As soon as the other team gets a free hit or side in, the forwards on your team quickly form a ring around the hitter. All players must be five yards away from the hitter. The forwards set up in a low defensive position, with their weight on the balls of their feet and their sticks down on the ground. The lower you are in your stance and the more ground you cover with your stick, the better your chances of blocking the hit. Make sure that your stick is angled toward the ground so the ball doesn't deflect up into the air.

The two inners are in front of and to the left and right of the hitter. The left and right wing must keep an eye for long, flat passes and cut them off if the hitter is looking to switch fields. During a side in, the

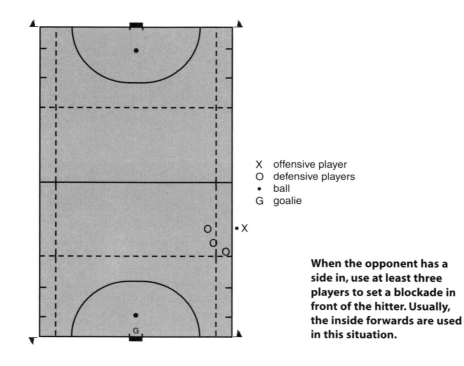

X   offensive player
O   defensive players
•   ball
G   goalie

When the opponent has a side in, use at least three players to set a blockade in front of the hitter. Usually, the inside forwards are used in this situation.

wing on the side of the field where the ball is being hit in covers that sideline. She is straight down the sideline from where the hit is being taken in a low defensive position. Her stick covers the space in front of her legs and is off to the right side of her body so the toe of her stick touches the sideline. This prevents the hitter from sending a strong forward pass down the sideline. Midfielders cover the spaces behind and between the forwards (about five to 10 yards behind them). Backs block up the deeper spaces behind the mids and are alerted to players who are moving downfield.

During free hits in the midfield areas, it is important to cover space, not individual players. Once the ball moves into the defensive 25 area, then it is time to mark up. But in the transitional area of the field, where most free hits and side ins occur, blocking up the space is the priority.

LONG HITS

When your team hits the ball over its own defensive end line, the offensive team gets a long hit. The long hit is taken from the sideline hash mark five yards up from the end line on the side of the field where the ball was hit out of play.

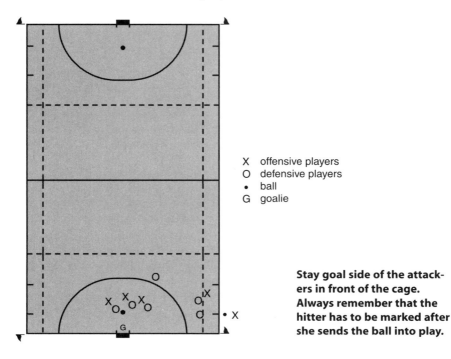

X offensive players
O defensive players
• ball
G goalie

Stay goal side of the attackers in front of the cage. Always remember that the hitter has to be marked after she sends the ball into play.

All players mark up when the other team gets a long hit. One player—usually the midfielder playing on the side of the field where the hit is being taken—covers the hit in. She stands on the circle line opposite where the hit is being taken, facing the hitter. Stand in a low defensive position.

The forward on that same side covers the hitter's short back pass, who is positioned near the 25. Everyone else marks up all players in the 25-yard area, giving attention to the most dangerous players in the circle and in front of the cage first. Once the hit in is taken, the midfielder marks the hitter, and the forward stays on the back who was in the back pass position.

DEFENSIVE CORNERS

When your team commits a foul in the defensive circle, the other team gets a penalty corner and the defense plays with only five players for a limited time. All other players on the defending team, except the goalie and four defenders, must run back to the 50-yard line. They stay there until the other team hits the ball into play.

The defenders stand behind the end line—two in the cage with the goalie and two outside the post closest to the hitter. All sticks and feet must be behind the end line. The offensive team sets up with one player hitting the ball in at the hash mark on the end line 10 yards from the closest goalpost. The hit in can be taken on either side of the goalpost at either hash mark. Other offensive players are positioned around the circle.

The Right Trail

The defender outside the cage closest to the hitter is a right trail. Her main priority once the hit out is taken is to mark the hitter, who will be rushing in on the cage.

The Fly

The defender next to the right and closest to the post is the fly. She sprints out to the shooter—the offender who receives the hit in—as soon as the ball is hit into play. The fly rushes directly to the ball, holding her stick in her right hand. A strong right-hand grip at the top of the stick with the flat side facing forward gives the best reach. In addition, it leaves your left arm free to pump while you sprint.

As you approach the shooter, extend your stick out to the right with the flat side facing forward. Sprint to the left of the shooter so your body is out of the line of the shot but your stick is in its path and on the ground. Keep as much of your stick on the ground as possible by staying low. The fly's job is to get the ball away from the shooter before she has a chance to shoot or to deflect her shot out of the circle with her stick. As soon as the ball is hit into play, the players who were sent to the 50-yard line sprint back to the circle to mark.

The Left Trail

The player inside the cage and behind the end line closest to the fly is the left trail. She runs two steps behind the fly and to the left. If the shooter decides to pass the ball off to her right, the trail is there to keep the pressure on.

The Post

The last defender in the cage—the one who is farthest from the ball—covers the left post opposite from where the hit in is taken. She stands right behind the goalie and guards the far post.

The post's job is to cover the ground inside the cage next to the post. When the ball is hit into play, take a step forward so you are in front of the goal line. Feel the left post with your shoulder to guarantee there is no space between you and the post. Keep your stick on the ground and your eyes on the ball.

Above: The defender outside the cage is called the right trail. She marks the hitter. The defender next to her is the fly. She sprints out to defend the shooter. The next defender on the right side of the goalie is the left trail. She runs a few steps behind and to the left of the fly. The last defender is called the post. She covers the area inside the cage next to the post. Next page: As soon as the ball is hit, sprint out to defend your positions.

These positions are critical for the initial shot. Once the first shot is taken and the goalie clears the ball out, all defenders mark up the most dangerous players.

DRILLS AND GAMES

3v2 with Recovery

Players: Five plus goalie
Equipment: Sticks, ball, cone, cage
Distance: 50 yards

Two defenders stand on the 25-yard line, one on the left side of the field and one in the center. The goalie is in the cage. Place one cone on the right side of the field on the 40-yard line. Three forward players stand on the 50-yard line at the right, center, and left positions, all facing the defense.

The defender on the left hits the ball out to the right forward (left, facing the defense—opposite side where the cone is). As soon as she hits the ball, the other defender sprints to the cone on the 40 and back, recovering to help her teammate defend.

While she is running, the other defender is a 3v1 situation and must be smart and patient, keeping the dribbler in front of her and staying parallel to the other forwards who are moving down the field. As the recovering defender comes back into play, she calls to her teammate to let her know she's back to help out. When she recovers, the pressuring defender can take a more aggressive approach to get the ball. The offense receives the ball and moves—with dribbling or passes—to the cage.

3v2 No Recovery

Players: Five plus goalie
Equipment: Sticks, ball, four cones, cage, and goalie equipment
Distance: 25 yards

Set up two five-yard wide goals with the cones on the far left and far right sides of the 25-yard line. Two defenders start in the circle. The goalie is in the cage. Three offense start facing the defense at the 25-yard line in left, center, and right positions. One offender has the ball. The offense begins working the ball into the circle with passes and dribbling techniques. The outnumbered defense must use pressure/cover and communication to force the offense out of the circle and get the ball from them. When the defense gets the ball, they send a strong hit up the field and out toward the closest sideline. The goal is to send that pass through the five-yard goals set up on the 25. These goals are outlets; in a game, this would be a pass to a wing for an offensive transition. The defense may also dribble through the cones if they get the ball outside the circle and close to the 25.

Every time the defense gets a ball through their goals—by passing or by dribbling—they get a point. The offense receives a point every time they score on the goalie in the circle.

Pressure/Cover in Circle

Players: Seven
Equipment: Sticks and ball
Distance: 15-yard circle

Five players stand in a circle with a 15-yard diameter. Two defenders are in the middle of the circle. One of the five offensive players on the circle starts with the ball. She passes the ball to her teammates around the circle, with the ultimate goal of making a through pass straight across the circle.

The defense is working pressure/cover angles to prevent all passes—in particular, the dangerous through pass—from happening. One defender pressures the girl with the ball. The cover player calls out which direction to force the pass; if you want to force the ball left, stand more to the right of the dribbler.

As the ball moves around the circle, the pressure/cover roles switch, depending on who is closer to the ball. Pressure/cover roles must communicate with one another by calling out what role they are in every time the ball is passed. Whoever is going to pressure the dribbler always calls out "pressure" or "ball." Cover shouts out, "cover," and directs her pressuring teammate.

When a pass is intercepted, the defense gets one point. Every time a through pass is completed, the offense gets one point. Play for seven minutes.

Focus on the Cover

Players: Six
Equipment: Sticks, ball, cones
Distance: 30-yard square

Place the cones in the corners of a 30-yard square. Draw an imaginary line through the middle of the field and split your group into two teams of three players each. The two teams face each other in the square, each on its respective side. One player on each team is in the cover position and stands on the back end line. The other two are pressure players.

The two teams scrimmage each other with regular hockey rules. The cover role, however, can only come two yards off her end line. She is not allowed to play in the field. The cover role always works with whoever is pressuring the ball on her team. She tells them which way to force the ball and shouts out any other helpful directives.

Every time the ball is dribbled or passed over the end line a point is scored for that team. It does not count if it is an uncontrolled hit from the other side of the field. Play for 10 minutes.

Positioning Ball Side/Goal Side (Beginner to Advanced—Shots on Goal)

Players: Seven and goalie
Equipment: Sticks, balls, cage, goalie equipment
Distance: The circle

Five offensive players stand spread out around the circle, each with a ball. Two offense and one defense are in the circle. The player on the far right of the circle starts with the ball. The offense in the circle are positioned in front of the cage to receive a pass from her and deflect it into the goal. The defender is ball side/goal side of the most dangerous offensive player in the circle—the player closest to the ball.

The player on the circle takes a shot and the offense moves to get it into the goal. The defender and goalie must work together to stop this from happening and send the ball out of the circle. When a goal is scored or the ball is cleared out of the circle, the next player on the circle takes a shot and the play continues again. Continue until every player on the circle has taken a shot. In this drill, the defender is focusing on covering the most dangerous girl in the circle and staying ball side/goal side during circle play.

10
CONDITIONING

A stronger, well-conditioned athlete is a better athlete. Case closed. Do you want to run faster, stick harder, hit the ball with more power, gain better position by using your strength? If the answer is yes, it's time to start a conditioning program.

The stereotype that women are in uncharted waters when entering the weight room has also passed. Girls of all ages condition their bodies to enhance performance and reduce the risk of injury. To achieve maximum results as a field hockey player, you've got to train hard. This includes weight training, cardiovascular training, flexibility training, and agility training. Each type of training is necessary to become a complete player. Weight training increases swing speed and power, improves wrist strength, and enhances explosive running speed on the field. Flexibility training keeps you loose and limber. This enables you to stay fluid and rhythmic while the body is in motion. Cardiovascular training helps keep your legs strong throughout an entire game. There is a lot of running in field hockey, so cardiovascular training should be a major part of

Strength, endurance, and agility are essential to success during field hockey competition.

your body conditioning. All the stick skills in the world won't do you any good if you're gasping for air as you trail your opponent down the field. Finally, there is agility training. It works on your balance and improves quickness. Field hockey is a game of quick, explosive movements that require balance. Agility training allows you to execute your skills swiftly and from a balanced position.

FLEXIBILITY TRAINING

It's sensible to introduce conditioning with flexibility training. Whenever you engage in physical activity, start with stretching exercises. Prior to practices, games, or workouts, always stretch to perform effectively and avoid injury.

Before stretching, jog lightly for two to four minutes. This loosens your joints and muscles and acts as your body's wake-up call. Once you've finished jogging, begin stretching. Ideally, you want to hold each stretch for a few seconds until you feel the muscles relax. Then increase the stretch until you feel resistance again.

These stretching exercises start from the ankles and move upward. Refer to this routine each time you work out, practice, or play a game.

Ankle Stretch

Lift your foot off the ground and balance on one leg. Point your toe toward the ground and make circles with your foot to loosen the ankle joint. Make 10 circles and then switch feet. After completing two sets of 10, make counterclockwise circles with your feet 10 times.

The ankle stretch.

Calf and Achilles Tendon Stretch

Lean against a post, a wall, or a fence, with your hands pressed firmly against the object you're leaning on. Move one leg six to eight inches backward, keeping both feet flat on the ground. Bend the front knee forward and allow the heel of the rear foot to raise off the ground. Keep the toe of your rear foot on the ground. Hold the stretch for 10 seconds and then switch legs. Continue until you complete three sets of stretches for each leg.

Upper Hamstring Stretch

Lie flat on your back. Bend your left leg at the knee and raise it toward your midsection. Grab the shin of your left leg with both hands and pull into your midsection. Pull it up toward your chin as far as possible. Your right leg and back should remain as flat as possible on the ground. Hold the stretch for 10 seconds and then switch legs. Complete three sets for each leg.

Lower Hamstring Stretch

Standing erect with your feet close together, cross your right foot over your left foot and bend at the waist. Grab your ankles or feet (whatever your flexibility allows) with both hands. Hold the stretch for 10 seconds and switch. Try to increase your stretch with each set.

Quadriceps Stretch

Standing erect, bend your right leg at the knee so your right foot raises behind you. Reach down with your right hand and grab the instep of your right foot. Pull your foot up to your

The calf stretch.

The upper hamstring stretch.

The lower hamstring stretch.

The quadriceps stretch.

The torso stretch.

buttocks, while maintaining your balance on your left leg. Hold the stretch for 10 seconds and then relax and switch legs.

Torso Stretch

Sit on the ground with your legs stretched outward in front of you. Bend your right leg at the knee, slide your right foot inward toward your buttocks, and grab your right knee with both hands. Next, lift your right foot over your left leg and place it on the outside of your left knee. Put your right hand on the ground by your right side (for balance) and place your left on the outside of your right knee. Pull the knee to the left to feel a stretch in the right portion of your torso. Hold for 10 seconds and switch.

Lower Back Stretch

Lie flat on your stomach on the ground. Use both hands to push your upper body up off the ground, but keep your entire lower body (from the waist down) pressed against the ground. Hold this position for 10 seconds and then rest. Repeat this four or five times to stretch the lower back.

Upper Back Stretch

Holding your hands out in front of you, lock them together with your fingers. Raise your hands above your head and stretch your arms up toward the sky. Turn your hands over so your palms face the sky. Hold your arms up in this extended position for 15 seconds. Rest and repeat five times.

Shoulder Stretch

Lay your right arm across your chest. Grab your right elbow with your left hand and pull your right arm up and to the left. Hold the stretch for 10 seconds and then relax. Repeat the same exercise, this time pulling your left arm across your body. Stretch each arm for three sets.

Neck Stretch

Relax your neck and drop your head downward. Slowly roll your head in a clockwise motion, going around five times. Take a rest (so you don't get too dizzy) and then slowly roll it around in a counter-clockwise motion. Repeat each direction three times.

Triceps Stretch

Lift your right arm directly back over your right shoulder. Reach over your head with your left hand, grab your right elbow, and pull it back. Pull it back as far as you can go without experiencing pain. Hold the stretch for 10 seconds and switch arms. Stretch each tricep for three sets.

The shoulder stretch.

The triceps stretch.

Forearms Stretch

Extend your right arm out in front of you and turn your hand over so your palm faces the sky. Grab the fingers with your left hand and pull them down. Keep the right arm extended as you do this. Hold the stretch for 10 seconds and then switch arms. Next, allow the palm to face down and pull up on the fingers. Hold this stretch for 10 seconds and then switch. Repeat each stretch three times.

CARDIOVASCULAR TRAINING

Cardiovascular training is also referred to as endurance training. It builds stamina in your muscular and respiratory systems. It keeps your heart rate under control during competition, which allows you to play relaxed, on an even keel. Passing, receiving, dribbling, and shooting are skills that require a sense of touch and accuracy. If you're out of breath, you're not going to be able to perform these skills consistently or at your optimum skill level.

The importance of cardiovascular training cannot be stressed enough in field hockey. The bottom line is, if you're in better shape than your opponent, you will have a huge advantage. You'll be able to mark her tighter and deny her the ball on defense. You'll win more loose balls in the field. You'll be open for passes and scoring chances more frequently because your opponent will have difficulty keeping up with your runs.

Make the decision to get into peak condition for your field hockey season. Getting into good shape is 100 percent mental. Commit yourself to a training program and reap the benefits on the field. Never lose a battle because your competitor is in better shape.

Local fitness centers provide a variety of ways to build endurance. Aerobic classes, step class, Spinning, biking, and kickboxing classes are all enjoyable methods of achieving your goals. Fitness machines such as the Stairmaster and treadmills also offer excellent cardiovascular workouts. If you have access to a local gym, it will provide a great resource for you to fulfill your fitness needs. Joining a gym is highly recommended.

In addition to providing equipment, fitness centers offer trainers who can teach you proper technique. They're educated in devising fitness programs and can create a personal program to satisfy your individual needs. You can also pick up new training tips by observing the workouts of other gym members or even hitch up to a workout buddy. It's very beneficial to have a workout partner present to push you to work harder, especially on days that you're lacking enthusiasm.

There are plenty of other training methods to fulfill your cardiovascular training needs. Distance running can be performed on back roads, park trails, or outdoor tracks. Bicycling is another activity that builds stamina and leg strength. Sprint intervals improve speed, heighten reflexes, and build explosiveness—all traits that will be of great service to you on the hockey field.

Training Can Be Fun

Most young athletes grimace when cardiovascular or endurance training is mentioned, but it doesn't have to seem like a chore. Be creative and make it fun. Set up relay races where the losing team has to do sit-

Team sprints and relay races at practice can add zest to cardiovascular conditioning.

ups. Time your runs (both sprints and long distance) and compete with your teammates for the best time.

Many enjoyable recreational sports are perfect for cardiovascular training. Tennis, indoor soccer, Rollerblading, and racquetball are just a few sports that provide forms of cardiovascular training while you're competing. Swimming is another sport that builds strength and endurance.

When preparing for the field hockey season, sustain a cardiovascular training program that entails six days of training per week. Spend four days a week running distance and sprints. On the other two days, pick a recreational sport to mix things up. Adjust your workout regimen every couple of weeks. Constantly shocking or surprising the body always provides the best results.

WEIGHT TRAINING

University of Arizona conditioning coach Marc Hill once said, "Strength conditioning is not just simply for the benefit of getting big and strong, but also for being able to play at the highest level possible with as few injuries as possible." Hill makes two excellent points in this statement. By increasing your strength, you're making steps toward playing up to your maximum potential. That is what each player should aspire to. The other important point is that to perform well, you've got to be on the field. Weight training helps prevent injury. It strengthens muscle tissue, which protects ligaments and tendons. Without your health, you will be unable to contribute to your team on the field. Facing a great goal scorer can give you heartache, but an injury puts you on the sidelines and takes you completely out of competition.

CONSULT WITH AN EXPERT

Many young athletes have not been educated in weight training exercises. If you have never been given strength training instruction, seek out a certified trainer or speak to your coach. As beneficial as weight lifting can be, it can cause injury if the proper safety measures are not taken. In addition, improper technique can result in muscular strains and lead to chronic injury. Consult a professional to ensure safety and reap the maximum benefits from your hard work.

Strengthening the body means the entire body. Isolating a few areas of the body and building muscle in those regions is short-sighted. The legs, torso, abdominals, lower and upper back, shoulders, chest, arms, and wrists all need to be built up. Because you're a field hockey player, give more attention to the legs, torso, abdominals, and forearms. Those regions are extremely important to this particular sport. That doesn't mean the other muscle groups should be ignored, but the exercises for those mentioned areas should be intensified.

Below are some basic weight lifting exercises. They are designed to strengthen and tone muscles but not to build bulk. Building bulk can restrict your flexibility, which must be maintained. Depending on what you may or may not have access to, Nautilus and Universal weight machines can work as substitutes for free weights. Seek the advice of a coach or expert before initiating your weight lifting program.

Recommending a specific weight-training program is a delicate topic when dealing with young athletes. Every girl has a distinct body type, physically develops and matures at different stages of life, and maintains a particular muscular structure due to her individual genetic makeup. We're unable to give you an exact amount of weight for these exercises because too many factors such as age, strength, size, and weight are unknown. You and your trainer are responsible for determining the proper and safe amount of weight for your workouts. As you'll notice in the exercises that are recommended below, it's suggested that you complete 10 to 15 repetitions for each set. If you follow this guideline, you should be able to avoid using a weight that is

Push-ups are an excellent exercise that builds upper body strength. They improve strength in the chest, triceps, biceps, and shoulder regions.

Sit-ups increase strength in your abdominal muscles. Have a partner hold your feet while you work your abs.

too heavy. Beginners should increase strength through many repetitions rather than lifting heavy weights. As you mature physically and gain more strength, you can then increase the amount of weight and lower the number of repetitions. However, consult a certified trainer or coach before doing so.

Note: There are many types of strengthening exercises, far too many to list in this book. If you discover a program that includes exercises you don't recognize (or are not listed below), consult a certified trainer and request that he or she show you the proper technique.

Leg Extensions—Quadriceps Muscles

Seated on a leg-extension machine, hook the tops of your feet under the pads. Lock your ankles, but don't point your toes. Extend your legs up so your thighs are flexed and your toes point to the ceiling. Slowly lower the weight back down until it's just short of the starting position. This keeps pressure on your legs throughout the exercise. Continue for 10 to 15 repetitions.

Leg Curls—Hamstring Muscles

Lying face down on your stomach, lock your heels under the pads of the machine. Point your toes to the ground. Contract your gluteus maximus muscles and curl your legs up as far as you can. Isolate the hamstrings by keeping your hips and chest down on the bench. Lower the weight slowly to just short of the starting position. Continue for 10 to 15 repetitions.

Lunges—Gluteus Maximus Muscles

Holding dumbbells (approximately 15–20 pounds) in each hand down by your side, stand erect with your feet shoulder width apart. Take a forward stride approximately three feet long. As your stride lands, bend your knee and lower your rear knee almost to the floor. Push yourself back up to the starting position and repeat with the right leg. Continue for eight to 10 repetitions.

Leg Press—Quadriceps, Hip Flexor, and Buttocks

Sit on a leg press machine with the soles of your feet flat against the foot plate. Slowly lower the weight down until the top of your calves touch the bottom of your hamstrings. Slowly push back up and stop just before your knees lock. Continue for 10 to 15 repetitions.

Bent-Leg Sit-Ups—Abdominal Muscles

Lying on your back, bend your knees in and place the soles of your feet on the ground. Place your hands behind your head and curl up, bringing your chest up to your knees. Continue for 20 to 25 repetitions.

Bent-Leg Sit-Up Twists—Abdominal Muscles

Lie flat in the bent-leg sit-up position. As you curl up, twist so your left elbow touches your right knee. Lower yourself back down and alternate by touching your right elbow to your left knee. Continue for 15 to 20 repetitions.

Leg Lifts

Lying flat on your back, lift your legs up off the ground keeping both legs extended. Raise your legs until your buttocks lift off the ground. Lower your legs very slowly until they are about four inches from the ground. Continue for 15 to 20 repetitions.

Medicine Ball Hand-Offs—Torso and Abdominal Muscles

You'll need a partner for this exercise. Holding a medicine ball, stand back to back with your partner. Twist to your right as she twists to her left and hand her the ball. Immediately twist to the left and receive a pass back from your partner. After approximately 15 exchanges, switch directions and pass the ball off to your left.

V-Seat Pull-Ins—Lower Back Muscles

Seated on the floor, extend your legs out in front of you and place the soles of your feet up against the foot plates. Lean forward with your upper body to grab the handle grips with both hands. Return to the seated position and allow your knees to flex slightly. Pull the grips into your midsection and stick your chest out as your arms touch your midsection. Slowly allow the weight to return to the starting position.

Pull-Downs—Upper Back Muscles

Seated on the pull-down machine, grab the ends of the bar with both hands, palms facing forward. Tilt your head slightly forward and pull the bar down behind your head until it touches your neck. Let the bar slowly raise back up and then pull back down. Continue for 10 to 15 repetitions. To alter the exercise and isolate the upper back muscle region, flip your hands so that your palms face you. Pull the bar down in to the top of your chest and slowly return it to the starting position. Continue for 10 to 15 repetitions.

Bench Press—Pectoral Muscles

Lie face up on a weight bench with your feet flat on the ground. Grip the bar so your middle knuckles are pointed up to the ceiling. Each hand should be approximately three to four inches outside your shoulder. Lift the bar off the rack and hold it over your chest. Slowly lower the bar until it touches the upper region of your chest. Keep your elbows under the bar. Push the bar back up until near extension. Continue for 10 to 15 repetitions.

Biceps Curls—Biceps Muscles

Seated on the edge of a bench, hold a dumbbell in each hand. Rotate your wrists outward so your palms face forward. While maintaining an erect posture, slowly curl the dumbbell up near your collarbone. Lower the dumbbell back down and repeat the movement with your opposite arm. Repeat this 10 to 15 times with each arm.

Triceps Pull-Downs—Triceps Muscles

Standing at a pull-down machine, grasp the bar with both hands spread slightly narrower than shoulder width apart. Use a forward grip so your palms face the floor. Push straight down on the bar until your arms nearly lock. Slowly let the bar return to the starting position. Continue for 10 to 15 repetitions.

Side Shoulder Raise—Shoulder Muscles

Stand straight up with your arms hanging down by your sides. Holding a light dumbbell in each hand, raise your arm out and up until it's parallel with the ground. When the dumbbell is at shoulder height, your palms should face the ground. Allow the dumbbell to slowly return to the starting position and raise the opposite arm. Continue each arm for 10 to 15 repetitions.

DON'T FORGET TO BREATHE

Breathing is very important when training with weights. The body needs oxygen to fuel working muscles. Proper breathing during an exercise is very simple. Inhale during the relaxed portion of the repetition, and exhale during the strenuous segment. For example, when doing pull-downs for the upper back muscles, inhale as your arms are moving upward, and exhale as you pull the weight back down behind your head. Inhale when you're relaxing and allowing the weight to return to the starting position, and exhale when you're pulling it back down.

If you don't breathe, you'll have less strength and energy to complete your sets. You may even become light-headed and out of breath at the end of a set. Breathe throughout the entire exercise.

AGILITY TRAINING

Making a recovery tackle, faking out and dribbling around a defender, and hitting a dive shot are examples of common plays that require agility. Speed allows a player to cover large amounts of territory in a small amount of time, but improving agility augments quickness, explosiveness, and the ability to change direction.

The following agility exercises are designed to improve your balance and quickness. They can be practiced on the hockey field. Coaches are often heard applauding players with a great first step, their ability to make sharp cuts and turns, or how fast a runner is able to accelerate. These exercises will help you develop those skills.

Lateral Line Jumps

Using the sideline, stand on the out-of-bounds side facing the goal. Place both feet together and position them so you're standing right next to the line. (Your feet are now parallel to the sideline.) Keeping both feet together, jump up and over the foul line, landing in the field of play. Without hesitation, jump back over to the out-of-bounds side and continue jumping back and forth for 30 seconds. Do your best to maintain balance. Count how many jumps you perform in 30 seconds and work to increase that number each time you train. This exercise improves leg strength, balance, and explosiveness.

Forward/Backward Line Jumps

Turn your feet so they are perpendicular to the sideline and you're facing the opposite sideline. Keeping your feet together, leap forward over the sideline into the field of play. Upon landing, immediately jump backward over the line and out-of-bounds. Continue jumping forward and backward for 30 seconds. Count how many jumps you perform in 30 seconds and work to increase that number each time you train. This exercise improves leg strength, balance, and explosiveness.

Horizontal line jumps are a simple way to improve agility and increase explosiveness in your legs.

Vertical line jumps are great for developing balance.

Four Corners

Use four cones to describe a square with a cone at each corner. Each side of the square should be approximately 20 yards in length. Starting at the bottom right corner of the square, jog straight to the top right corner cone. Once you reach the cone, shuffle sideways to the left along the top of the square. After reaching the top left corner cone, run backwards down the left side of the square until you arrive at the bottom left corner cone. Finally, sprint along the baseline of the square to return to the starting position. Continue this pattern until you've run four full circuits, then rest. This exercise builds endurance and improves overall agility and balance.

Pick-Ups

You'll need a partner and a hockey ball for this exercise. Face your partner and stand approximately 10 feet away from her. Your partner initiates the exercise by rolling the ball about six feet to your right. Shuffle-step to your right, field the ball with your hands, and then toss the ball underhand back to your partner. Quickly shuffle back as your partner rolls the ball six feet to the left of your starting point. Continue shuffling back and forth until you've completed 30 pick-ups. Pick-ups improve lateral movement and leg strength.

Following Orders

Stand out on the playing field or anywhere that gives you plenty of space. Face a coach or teammate and respond by moving in the direction of her command. Her job is to call out and point up, back, right, or left. If the caller yells "back," backpedal until you're given the next command. If she points to your left and yells "left," shuffle to the left until hearing the next command. Continue following orders for 45 seconds before resting. This exercise focuses on your ability to change direction and also builds endurance.

Bleacher Steps

You'll need a set of bleachers for this exercise. Stand at the base of the bleachers, raise your right foot, and place it on the first row. Your left foot remains planted on the ground as the ball of your right foot rests on the corner edge of the bleacher. This is the starting position. At the sound of a whistle or coach's call, interchange your feet as quickly as possible. Repeatedly exchange your feet, touching the front row of the bleachers with the bottom of your feet, "Left, right, left, right, left, right," and so on. Continue exchanging feet for 45 seconds, accumulating as many touches as possible. Keep track of your total number and attempt to beat that number each time. This exercise improves foot speed and quickness.

CONDITIONING PROGRAMS

How you train your body depends on the time of year and your personal goals. The off-season is the optimal time to build strength and increase speed. The lion's share of your work is performed at the fitness center or track, not on the hockey field. Your ultimate goal is to improve as a field hockey player, but during the off-season, concentrate on developing a better body to execute field hockey skills.

Exercise	Weight	Sets	Reps
DAY ONE			
Shoulder press	XX	3	8
Dumbbell bench press	XX	3	12
V-seat pull-ins	XX	2	12
Side shoulder raises	XX	2	10
Forearm curls	XX	burn	burn
Wall squats	XX	2	6
Leg curls	XX	2	12
Leg extensions	XX	2	12
Calf raises	XX	2	25
Abs (sit-ups)	XX	burn	burn
DAY TWO			
Bench press	XX	3	12
Power shrugs	XX	3	5
Dumbbell incline press	XX	3	10
Pull-downs	XX	3	10
Triceps extensions	XX	3	10
Biceps curls	XX	3	10
Forearms (wrist rolls)	XX	burn	burn
Abs (leg lifts)	XX	burn	burn
DAY THREE			
Leg press	XX	3	12
Squats	XX	3	12
Leg curls	XX	2	12
Lunges	XX	2	6
Calf raises	XX	2	25
Medicine ball passes	XX	3	15
Forearm curls	XX	burn	burn
Abs	XX	burn	burn

Once you move into the preseason, reduce your time spent at the gym and begin focusing on field hockey. Instead of four or five workouts per week, limit yourself to three sessions per week. Maintain your weight-training program, but adjust it by increasing the number of repetitions and decreasing the amount of weight. Cardiovascular, flexibility, and agility training exercises should be incorporated into practices by your coach. If insufficient time is spent in any of these areas, stay after practice and get your work in. Don't make the mistake of ignoring any facet of your conditioning program once preseason starts. If you do, your hard work in the off-season will be wasted.

During the season, do your best to maintain strength and fitness. Lift light weights two or three times per week for approximately 30 minutes. These are classified as maintenance workouts, designed to keep your muscles strong despite the wear and tear of a busy game schedule. The grind of practicing and playing every day causes the body to lose strength and explosiveness. Filtering in brief workouts helps to stave off weight loss and diminished muscle mass. Strenuous workouts are not recommended. Conserve your energy for competition.

Every player has a different body type, individual strength, and goals so there is not one universal workout that is best for everyone. On the previous page is a weight training workout program. Use this program as a foundation or guideline and then modify it to your needs and time of year. Set weights that are comfortable for you. This program is based on strength training three days per week. Always consult a fitness expert before starting to ensure that your program targets the goals you're striving to accomplish.

Note: When the number of sets and reps is listed as "burn," that means you should continue performing the exercise until you burn out.

NUTRITION

You could own the sweetest car in school, but unless there's gas in the tank, it's not going to be of much service to you. The same theory applies when it comes to athletics. Athletic ability becomes a nonfactor if your body is devoid of nutrients. Proper nutrition enables you to train or compete at the highest level possible. Eating the right foods fuels the body to perform at its best.

Eating properly allows you to maintain a desirable body weight, stay physically fit, and establish optimal nerve-muscle reflexes. So is there something you should eat every day that will satisfy these needs? Yes and no. There is not one specific food that gives you everything you need. Your body needs a variety of nutrients—proteins, carbohydrates, fats, vitamins, minerals, and water—to energize your body. A balanced diet provides these nutrients. The nutrient surpluses in some foods compensate for the nutrient deficiencies in others.

To maintain a balanced diet, use the four basic food groups as your guideline. A combination of foods from the dairy group, meat and poultry group, fruit and vegetable group, and bread and pasta group provides a basic structure from which to devise your dietary plan. Below is a table that lists the food groups, the major nutrients each supplies, and the recommended amount for teenage athletes.

Food Group	Major Nutrients	Daily Servings
Dairy	Calcium, protein, vitamin A, riboflavin	3 servings
One serving is 8 ounces of milk, 8 ounces of yogurt, 1 1/2 ounces of cheese		
Meat/Poultry	Protein, thiamin, riboflavin, iron, niacin, zinc	2 to 3 servings
One serving is 3 ounces of lean meat (poultry, pork, fish, beef), 2 eggs, 1 cup of cooked beans or peas, 4 tablespoons of peanut butter		
Fruit and Vegetable	Vitamin A, C, and many other vitamins and minerals	5 to 7 servings
One serving is 1/2 cup of cooked vegetables, 1/2 cup of chopped vegetables, 1 whole fruit (apple, orange, banana), 1/2 grapefruit, 6 ounces of juice, 1/2 cup of berries		
Bread and Pasta	Complex carbohydrates, protein, B vitamins, iron	6 to 11 servings
One serving is 1 slice of bread, 1/2 English muffin, 1 small roll or biscuit, 1/2 cup of cooked rice or pasta, 1 ounce of breakfast cereal		

Cleaning Up Your Diet

Young athletes often have poor eating habits largely because they eat what tastes best. Teenagers don't regulate their food intake as closely as adults do because there are often no visible results from eating poorly. Heavy involvement in physical activities and high metabolism negate the possibility of significant weight gain, giving the impression that their bodies are healthy. However, a book cannot truly be judged by its cover. Although your body may appear physically fit, that doesn't mean it's receiving all of the nutrients it needs to perform at its maximum potential.

Good nutrition is not just about eating the right things. It also requires you to stop eating the wrong things. If you are an athlete who wants to improve your diet, follow these five rules.

Avoid junk food—Tempering temptation is often difficult, but you've got to exhibit willpower if you're seeking results. Avoid snacks like cookies, potato chips, and cheese fries. Instead, keep some pretzels, bagels, and fresh fruit available.

Decrease your dairy products—Dairy products are one of the major food groups, and it is suggested to include a mild amount of dairy (three servings) in your daily diet. Keep it at that. Do not feed your hunger with cheeses, ice cream, or sour cream–filled baked potatoes. Skim milk, low-fat yogurt, and low-fat mozzarella cheese are adequate replacements.

Ease up on the soft drinks—Soda and imitation fruit drinks are full of calories and provide very little supplements. They fail to quench your thirst or replenish your body with the energy it needs. Stick with water and natural fruit juices.

Drive past the drive-thru—Fast-food restaurants offer foods loaded with fat. If you must stop at a fast-food restaurant, look for menu items that are grilled and request that they leave the mayonnaise and secret sauce for the next customer.

Eliminate heavy toppings—Popular toppings such as butter, cheese, mayonnaise, heavy dressing, sour cream, and the like may add flavor to your meal, but they add even more fat grams. Fat-free dressing, mustards, vinaigrette, or low-fat margarine provide options to retrain your taste buds.

Eating Before Competition

Eating the right thing at the right time can greatly benefit your competitive prowess. Your goal is to supply your body with enough fluids and energy to enable you to battle as hard as you can for as long as you need. Complex carbohydrates such as pasta, baked potatoes, toast, and cereals are highly recommended. These should be consumed approximately three hours before competition. Keep the portions small so that your meal is easily digestible. Because your emotions are riding high entering a game, your digestive processes may be slowed. Do not eat foods that contain a lot of fat, and avoid sugary foods as well. Fats are digested very slowly and can make you feel sluggish. Sweets such as candy bars, soda, or honey may raise your blood-sugar level and reduce your energy level.

All-day tournaments can put you in a precarious position. Drinking plenty of fluids before and throughout the day is the most important issue to carry out. Consume a cup of cool water every 20 minutes during competition and 2–3 cups each hour after competition. Eat a meal heavy in carbohydrates the evening before competition, and feed yourself with snacks that are high in starch throughout the day's events. A box of granola bars is a smart item to pick up en route to the tournament.

DO I NEED TO TAKE VITAMIN OR MINERAL SUPPLEMENTS?

Athletes and parents of athletes are increasingly confronted with the issue of dietary supplements. The questions often raised are, "Will my athletic talents benefit from taking supplements?" and "If I'm not taking supplements, am I at a disadvantage to those who are taking supplements?"

Provided you work hard at your game, conditioning your body, and eating properly, there is no need for vitamin or mineral supplements. Increasing nutritious foods to meet increased energy expended will supply more than enough vitamins and minerals. Experts concur that the basis of good nutrition is a well-balanced diet, and vitamin and mineral supplements are no substitute for one. Excessive amounts of supplements taken over a prolonged period of time can prove to be harmful.

FIELD HOCKEY RESOURCES

http://www.usfieldhockey.com is the official website of the U.S. Field Hockey Association, the governing body of field hockey in America. The website provides educational and participation information to players, coaches, and officials, including information on the rules and regulations of field hockey, national teams and tournaments, and field hockey programs and camps.

For more information, contact:
U.S. Field Hockey Association
One Olympic Plaza
Colorado Springs, CO 80909
Phone: 719-866-4567

http://www.hockeytrainer.nl/eng provides training tips to field hockey coaches, as well as diagrams, video clips, and articles on training. The site also features a message board where coaches can post their field hockey questions.

http://www.hockeypoint.com is an online field hockey magazine providing news and stats on high school and college field hockey competition. Contact HockeyPoint via e-mail at michael@hockeypoint.com or call 877-326-9217.

http://www.obo.co.nz is the website of OBO, producer of goal keeping equipment. In addition to an online store, this site has an online expert to answer goal keeping questions.

For more information, contact:
OBO Goal Keeping
20 Sutton Place

P.O. Box 1782
Palmerston North
New Zealand
Phone: +64 6 356 6060
Fax: +64 6 356 3939
E-mail: joan@obo.co.nz

http://www.ncaa.org/sports/field_hockey is the field hockey page of the NCAA, the governing body of American intercollegiate athletics. This site includes team rankings, schools that sponsor teams, championship forms and handbooks, as well as all-season and championship information.

For more information, contact:
The National Collegiate Athletic Association
700 W. Washington Street
P.O. Box 6222
Indianapolis, IN 46206-6222
Phone: 317-917-6222
Fax: 317-917-6888

FURTHER READING

Adelson, Bruce. *The Composite Guide to Field Hockey.* Philadelphia, Pa.: Chelsea House Publishers, 2000.

Anders, Elizabeth (with Sue Meyers). *Field Hockey Steps to Success.* Champaign, Ill.: Human Kinetics Publishers, 1999.

Axton, W. F., and Wendy Lee Martin. *Field Hockey.* Indianapolis, Ind.: Masters Press, 1993.

Cannella, Stephen. "Scorecard/Field Hockey: Been There, Done That." *Sports Illustrated,* November 2, 1998, p. R7.

Field Hockey News. The official publication of the USFHA. October/November 2001.

Fong, Donna, ed. *Coach's Collection of Field Hockey Drills.* West Point, N.Y.: Leisure Press, 1982.

Hockey News The official publication of the USFHA. August/September 2001.

John, Jenny. *Field Hockey Handbook.* North Vancouver, B.C.: Hancock House Publishers, 1980.

Kaplan, Ben. "Super Tips: Field Hockey." *Sports Illustrated for Kids,* October 1, 1995, p. 58.

Kentwell, Richard G. R. *Field Hockey Techniques and Tactics.* Brooklyn, Mich.: Sauk Valley Sports Supply, 1986.

Meyer, Meghan. "Field Hockey: Competition, Camaraderie: Players Young and Old Agree: There's No Other Sport Like It." *The Palm Beach Post,* November 24, 2000, p. 1B.

Pearlman, Jeff. "Spotlight: Leader of the Pack." *Sports Illustrated,* September 8, 1987.

Read, Brenda. *Advanced Hockey for Women.* London: Faber, 1976.

Rushin, Steve. "Five Nations/Indian Field Hockey: Reign on the Wan." *Sports Illustrated,* July 22, 1996, p. 170.

Ward, Carl. *Hockey.* New York: Sterling Publishing Company, 1989.

Weiner, Jay. "Not Just Another Olympic Record." *Minneapolis Star Tribune,* August 1, 1996, p. 01S.

Williams, Lee Ann. *Basic Field Hockey Strategy.* Garden City, N.Y.: Doubleday, 1978.

Woolum, Janet. "Chapter 3: Outstanding Women Athletes Who Influenced American Sports: Constable Applebee (Field Hockey)." *Volume 1, Outstanding Women Athletes: Who They Are and How They Influenced Sports in America.* Phoenix, Ariz.: Oryx Press, 1992.

INDEX